Central Asia

Central Asia

Economy, Environment and Culture

Mohammad Shafi

RAWAT PUBLICATIONS
Jaipur • New Delhi • Bangalore • Mumbai • Hyderabad • Guwahati

ISBN 81-316-0060-2

Published by
Prem Rawat for **Rawat Publications**
Satyam Apts., Sector 3, Jawahar Nagar, Jaipur 302 004 (India)
Phone: 0141 265 1748 / 7006 Fax: 0141 265 1748
E-mail: info@rawatbooks.com
Website: www.rawatbooks.com

New Delhi Office
4858/24, Ansari Road, Daryaganj, New Delhi 110 002
Phone: 011-23263290

Also at Bangalore, Mumbai, Hyderabad and Guwahati

Typeset by Rawat Computers, Jaipur
Printed at Chaman Enterprises, New Delhi

Contents

Acknowledgments

I wish to express my deep sense of gratitude to M.J. Wise of the London School, London University, for his inspiration in the writing of this book. His advice was an asset to me.

I am thankful to Azizmuddin Qureshi and Salahuddin Qureshi for extending necessary facilities in the Department of Geography for writing this book. Thanks are due to Shakeel Ahmad, Librarian, M.A. University Library for providing me the material which I needed promptly, while writing the book.

I would also like to express my sincere thanks to Kaneez Talat of departmental library for providing me relevant material the book.

Special thanks are due to Najamuddin of the library for extending full facilities to me in respect of valuable material in writing this book. Thanks are also due to Mohd Javed, who abundantly helped me in the cartographic work of the book.

Khawaja Molaim Ahamd, who served the department in a distinguished manner and has now retired, was most helpful to me in the typing of the manuscript. I express my gratitude to Syed Hilal Nasir in the Department of Biochemistry and also to

Bilqees Bano, who patiently and painstakingly typed the manuscript on the computer.

Although it is not necessary to thank one's own kith and kin, nonetheless, I am thankful to all the members of my family for providing me supporting and stimulating surroundings for writing the book.

Mohammad Shafi

Preface

The need for writing a book on Central Asia arose because there is no systematic book on this region which constitutes a bridge between the East and the West. The region consists of five states, viz., Kazakhstan, Turkmenistan, Uzbekistan, Tajikistan, and Kyrgyzstan, formerly part of erstwhile Soviet Union and now independent republics. There are numerous ethnic nationalities living in each state, but the declared policy of each state is secularism.

Among the five states, Kazakhstan is the biggest one (2,717,300 sq km) in area and Uzbekistan is the most populous (26,593,000). The combined area of all the states is about 0.4 million sq km and the combined population in mid-2005 was about 60 million.

Although half the region is desert, the two rivers – the Amu and the Syr Darya – constitute the lifeline of the area, provide extensive irrigation and have made Central Asia as the fourth largest producer of cotton in the world. However, the excessive irrigation has produced adverse environmental consequences in the critical shrinkage of the Aral Sea wherein the rivers discharge their water.

Besides abundant oil and gas resources, Central Asia is a storehouse of minerals like ferrous and non-ferrous metallic minerals, iron ore, copper, nickel, bauxite, lead, zinc, manganese, chromite, titanium, uranium, tungsten, silver and gold. Its economy is gradually being transformed – as from nomadic herding it has taken up sedentary agriculture and produces large quantities of food grains, including wheat and rice, and a large variety of vegetables and fruits. Industrial development, based on food processing industries and metallic minerals, has also taken place rapidly. Kazakhstan has a stockpile of nuclear armaments.

Central Asia has a bright future as the states have a sizeable export and import system but the key word in its future development is sustainability.

1

Overview

Central Asia has five Independent Republics, each of which is characterized by specific ethnic identity, yet they share a common culture and history. These Republics are (1) Turkmenistan between the Caspian Sea and the Amu Darya, (2) Uzbekistan which runs from Aral Sea (an inland lake) to the Fergana basin, (3) Tajikistan which embraces the high plains and mountain ranges of the Pamirs, (4) Kyrgyzstan with lofty mountain ranges, and (5) Kazakhstan having broad expanse of desert that runs from the Caspian Sea to the border mountain of China (Figure 1).

Central Asian Republics present a fascinating landscape on the map of Asia. They were formerly part of the erstwhile Soviet Union, but after the dissolution of Soviet Union they became Independent Republics. The northern boundary is formed by Kazakhstan and the southern boundary is formed by the borders of Iran and Afghanistan.

The region consists of a variety of features: extensive low sandy desert in the west and north-west, the mountain zone with some of the highly glaciated ranges in the east, the Pamir plateau called the 'roof the world' and the two rivers, Syr and

Figure 1
Central Asia States

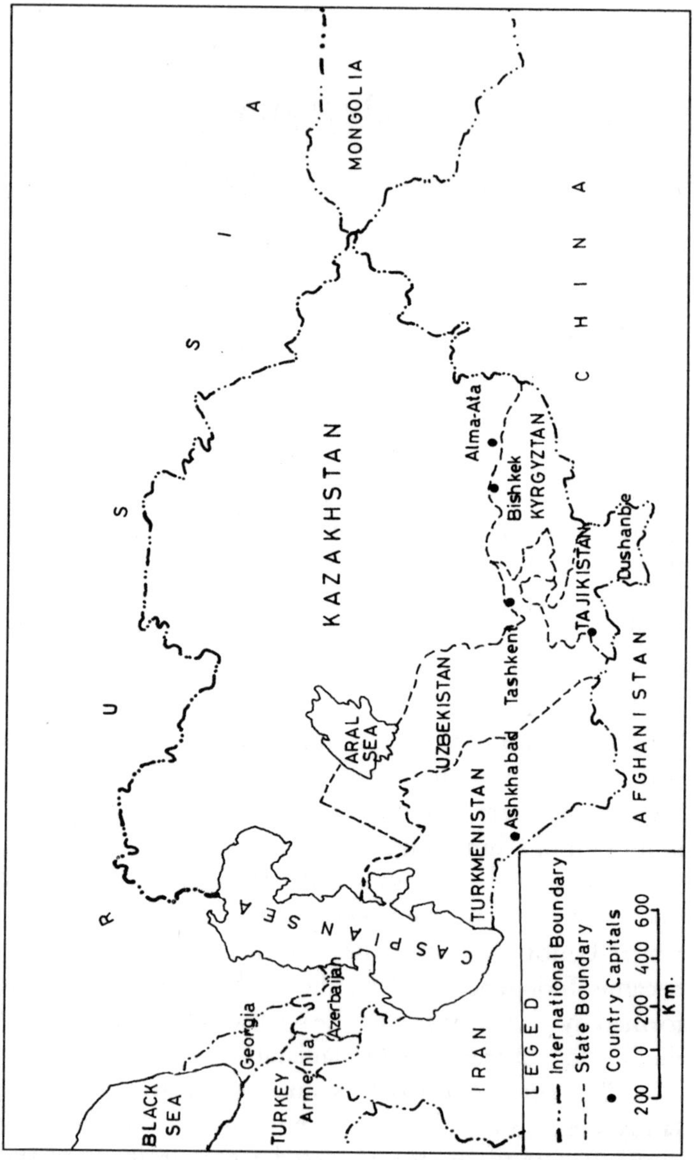

Figure 2
Central Asian States (Area in Percentage)

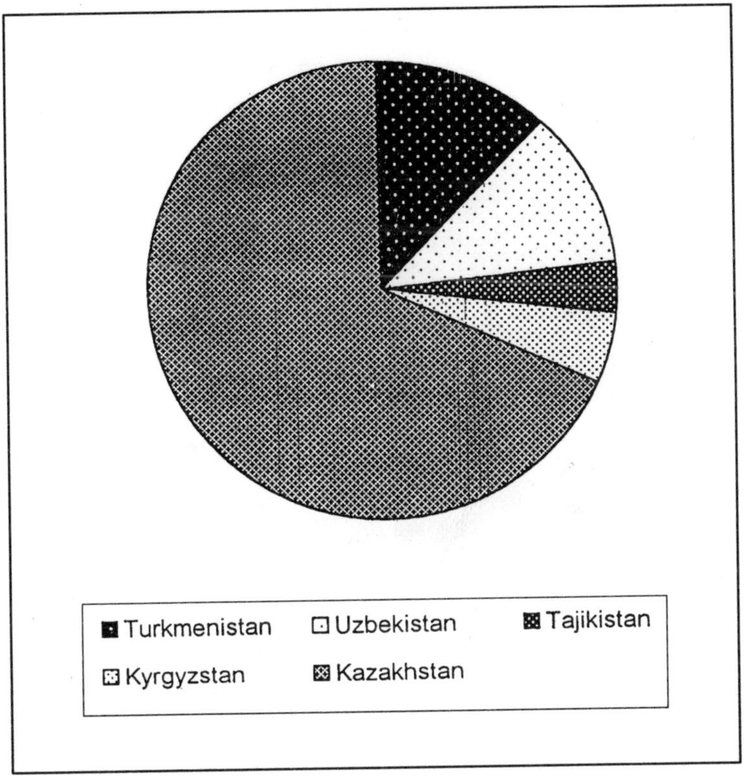

Amu Darya which are the lifeline of the region and drain into an inland lake – the Aral Sea.

The biggest state which occupies more than twice the combined area of all the four states is Kazakhstan and the smallest state is Tajikistan (Table 1 and Figure 2). The state, which has the highest population is Uzbekistan containing about 45.39 per cent (2004) of the total population of five states or 83 per cent (2004) of the total population of four states taken together, and the state having the least population is Turkmenistan (Figure 2a).

Figure 2a

Population of Central Asian States, 2004 (in Percentage)

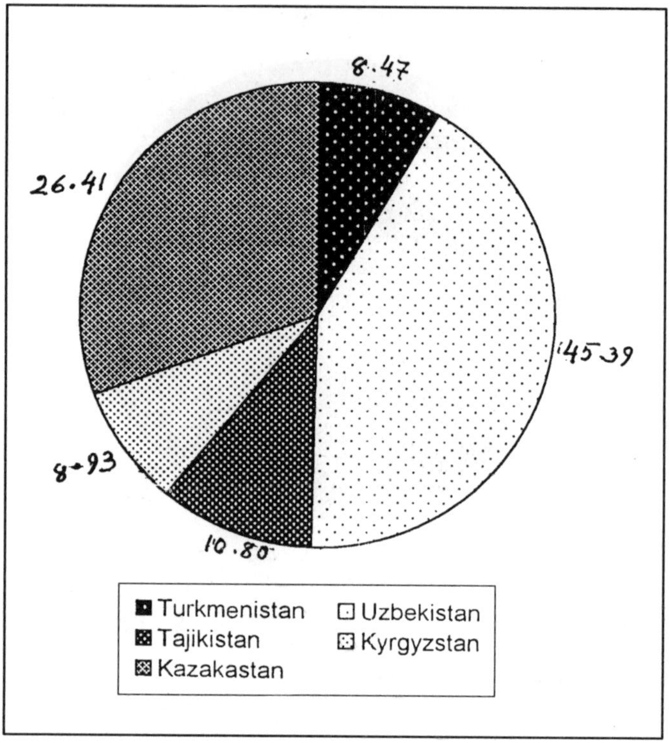

Table 1

Central Asian States

	(area in percentage)
Turkmenistan	12.23
Uzbekistan	11.20
Tajikistan	3.58
Kyrgyzstan	4.97
Kazakhstan	68.02

Sources: The percentage of each state has been computed by the author.

It would be worthwhile to examine briefly the historical evolution of these states (Figure 1).

Turkmenistan

It was in April 1918 that Turkmenistan was established as an autonomous Turkistan Soviet Socialist Republic. In October 1942, the name was changed to Turkmen Soviet Republic, and the Communist Party of Turkmen (CPT) reigned supreme. In August 1990, the Turkmen Supreme Soviet adopted a

Figure 3

Turkmenistan: Population by Ethnic Group, 1993 (in Percentage)

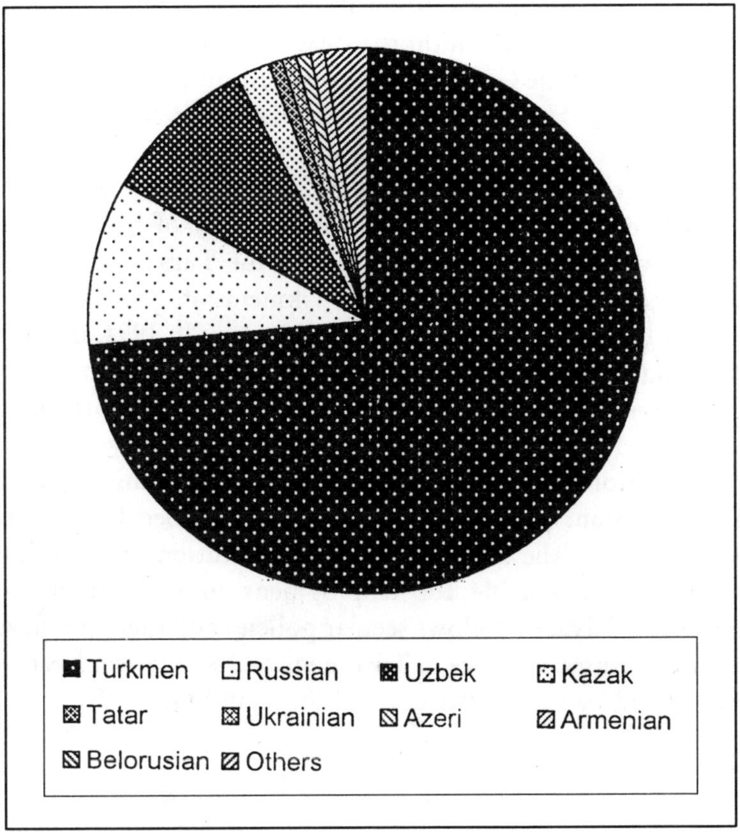

resolution declaring the state a sovereign republic free from nuclear and chemical weapons. The state further declared that it shall determine its own social and political system and can secede from the USSR. In October 1990 Niyazov was elected as the President of the state and in December 1991, CPT was changed to Democratic Party of Turkmenistan (DPT) with Niyazov as its Chairman. On 26 October 1991, there was a national referendum at which complete independence was voted for and on October 27, the name Turkmen SSR was changed to Republic of Turkmenistan and a new state emblem, flag and national anthem were adopted. On December 21, 1991 it joined the Commonwealth of 10 Independent States (CIS). In June 1992, Niyazov's authority was increased by appointing him as Head of the Government (Prime Minister) in addition to his position as Head of the State. He was also to act as Supreme Commander of the Armed Forces. In mid-December 1992 Niyazov was awarded the rank of General, further enhancing his authority. In 1993, the Caspian Sea port of Krasnovodsk was renamed Turkmenbashy (Head of the Turkmen). In 1995 December the title of 'Hero of Turkmenistan', the country's highest honour was conferred upon Niyazov In 1994, the term of President Niyazov was extended by the Majlis upto 2002 so that Niyazov could complete his programme of prosperity announced by him in 1993.

Mention should be made of two ethnic minorities in Turkmenistan: Russian 10 per cent and Uzbec 8 per cent. According to the Turkmenistan Constitution, only ethnic Turkmen are eligible for employment in state enterprise. However, Niyazov follows secular policies and there has never been any ethnic violence in Turkmenistan. Secularism has been guaranteed by the Constitution (Table 2 and Figure 2).

Table 2
Turkmenistan Population by Ethnic Groups (1993 Census)

(in percentage)

Turkmen	73.3
Russian	9.8
Uzbek	9.0
Kazak	2.0
Tatar	0.9
Ukrainian	0.8
Azeri	0.8
Armenian	0.8
Belorusian	0.2
Others	2.4

Uzbekistan

Uzbekistan was part of the erstwhile Soviet Union. It was a part of Turkistan Soviet Socialist Republic in 1918 and the Soviet Union exercised full control over it. On October 27, 1924, Uzbek Soviet Socialist Republic was proclaimed, and it included the Tajik Republic until 1929, but later Tajik was separated from Uzbek and Uzbek became a separate Republic still under Soviet control. In 1990, elections were held on the 500 seats of Uzbek Supreme Soviet and the legislature elected Islam Karimov to the newly created post of executive President. It was in August 1991, following the unsuccessful coup in Moscow that Uzbekistan declared itself independent and its name was changed to Republic of Uzbekistan and Communist Party of Uzbekistan (CPU) was designated as Peoples Democratic Party of Uzbekistan (PDRU) with Islam A. Karimov as its leader and president. In December 1991, Uzbekistan joined the Commonwealth of Independent States (CIS), and again a direct Presidential election was held in which Islam Karimov was elected by an overwhelming majority.

Figure 4
Uzbekistan: Population by Ethnic Group (Census 1989)
(in Percentage)

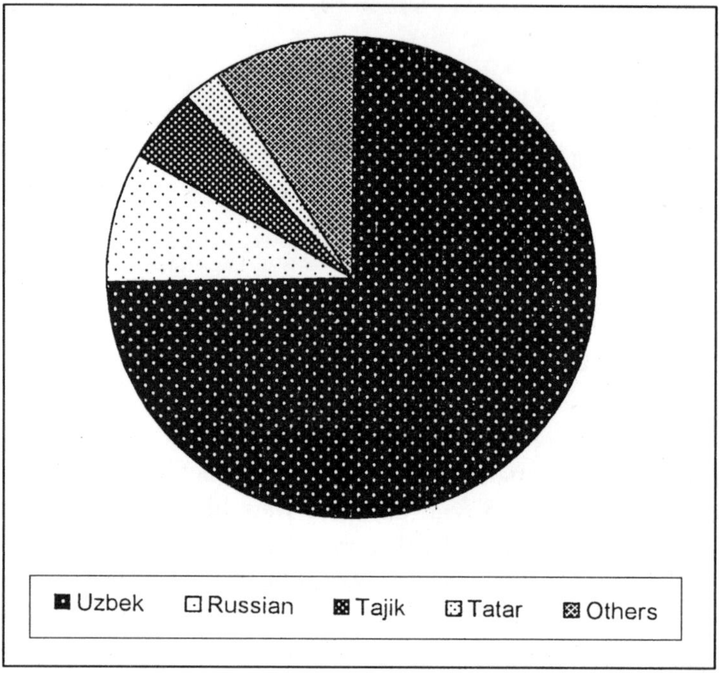

The new constitution of Uzbekistan guarantees secularism as well as democratic multiple party systems, freedom of expression and protection of human rights.

The Uzbeks constitute 71.4 per cent of the total population. The other ethnic minorities are Russians, Tajiks and Tatars (Table 3 and Figure 4).

In the year, after the dissolution of USSR, Uzbekistan experienced outbreaks of inter-ethnic strifes. The strife has been between the Uzbeks and the Turk minority. Unemployment and shortage of housing were the main reasons for such strifes. Uzbeks are the most dominant tribes and constitute almost three-fourths of all the ethnic tribes (Table 3 and Figure 4).

Table 3
Uzbekistan: Population by Ethnic Groups (Census 1989)

(in percentage)

Uzbek	71.4
Russian	8.3
Tajik	4.7
Tatar	2.4
others	9.1

Tajikistan

The Tajik was constituted as a separate ethnic group in the 18th century AD. They led a sedentary life and spoke Persian. In 1918 the northern part of their territory came under Russian control. In 1924, the Tajik, Autonomous Soviet Socialist Republic (ASSR) was established as a part of Uzbek Soviet Socialist Republic, and in 1929, the Tajik Autonomous Soviet Socialist Republic was established, but in 1971 September, after prolonged negotiations and political upheavals, Tajikistan was proclaimed as an independent state, based on democratic principles. In November, 1991, Nabivev was elected President and took office in December 1991. However in early November 1992, Imamali Rakhmonov was appointed Chairman of the Supremes Soviet, a post equivalent to Head of State.

Tajikistan has been involved in civil war since 1993 and estimates vary between 20,000 and 1,00,000 people killed in the civil war in February 1993. Some point out that the main cause of the destabilization was the insurgency support by the Afghan *mujahidin* from across the border of Tajikistan. There have also been skirmishes along the Tajik-Afghan border. The continuing border conflict has been interpreted by some observers as being partly a fight for the control of drug smuggling routes as Tajikistan is a major channel for illicit drug (chiefly opium) from Pakistan, Iran and Afghanistan to Russia and Western Europe and the control of trade was a major factor

Figure 5

Tajikistan: Population by Ethnic Group (Census 1989)
(in Percentage)

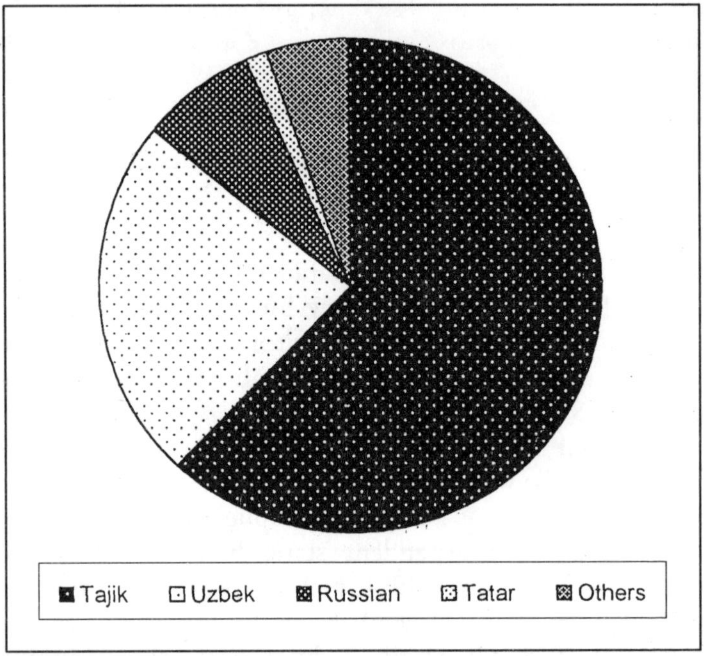

in the Tajik conflict. Today, Tajikistan's main problem is the skirmishes along the border with Afghanistan. The Tajik government became increasingly dependent on Russia for military assistance. In January 1993, Russia, Kazakhstan and Uzbekistan committed themselves to the defence of Tajikistan's southern frontier.

Relations with Afghanistan were strained by the apparent inability of the Afghan government to prevent mujahidin fighters and supply of arms from across the frontier into Tajikistan. However, as hostilities continued up to mid-1996, the Tajik government temporarily closed the border with Afghanistan. The victory of Taliban forces in Afghanistan in 1996, threatened to destabilize the delicate situation in

Tajikistan and as Talibans increased their territorial gains in northern Afghanistan there was increasing concern in Tajikistan that there might be an influx of large number of refugees.

The Tajik constitute 63 per cent of population, the Uzbek 24 per cent and Russians 8 per cent. The majority of the Tajiks are adherents to Islam was in November 6, 1994 that Imamali S. Rakhmonov was elected President by popular vote (Table 4 and Figure 5).

Table 4

Tajikistan Population by Ethnic Groups (Census 1989)

(in percentage)

Tajik	62.3
Uzbek	23.5
Russian	7.6

Kyrgyzstan

The forefathers of Khirghis, who were settled in the upper reaches of Yenisei River in the 10th century AD, migrated to the Tien-Shan region in the 13th century, as a result of the establishment of the Mongol empire. Soviet power was established in Kyrgyzstan by 1919 and it was in 1936 that the Khirghis Soviet Socialist Republic was established. In 1993, the Supreme Soviet guaranteed basic human rights and declared the Khirghis Republic to be a secular democratic state. Khirghisia established good relation with Arab and other Muslim states, in particular Turkey, with which it shares close ethnic, cultural and linguistic ties. Askaar Akayev became President of the state in 1990 and re-elected in 1991. Although Islam is the dominant religion, Kyrgyzstan continues to be a secular state.

The Kyrgyzstan government intensified controls along the border with Tajikistan in an attempt to prevent further infiltration by Tajik groups and Kyrgyzstan had to take extra precaution owing to the increase of drug trafficking across the border.

Figure 6

Kyrgyzstan: Principal Ethnic Groups (1989 Census) (in Percentage)

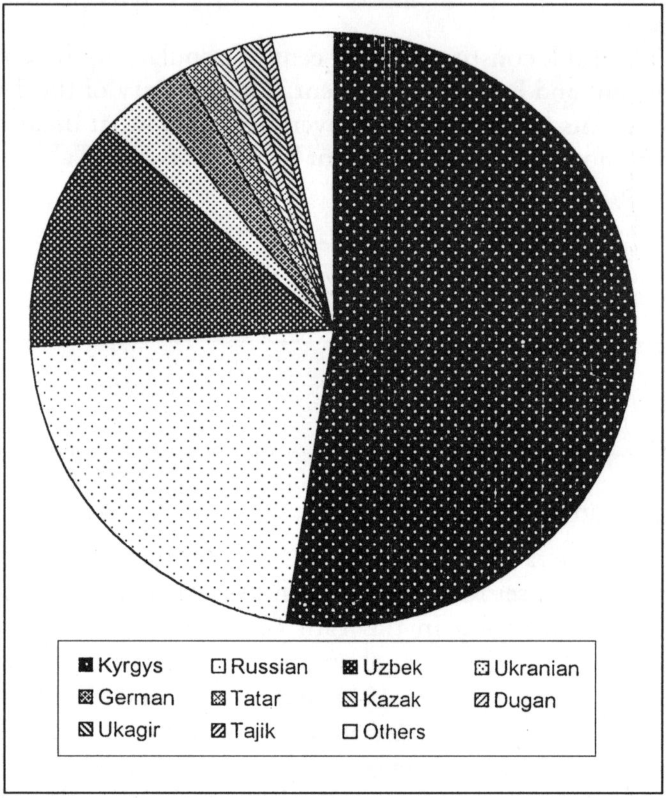

Half of the population of Kyrgyzstan consists of Kyrgys. Russians and Uzbek constitute 21.5 and 12.9 per cent respectively. These two are the major ethnic minorities (Table 5 and Figure 6).

Kazakhstan

Kazakhstan is peopled by the tribes who have descended from Mongol and Turkie tribes. These tribes settled in Kazakhstan in the first century BC.

Figure 7

Kazakhstan: Principal Groups (1994 Census) (in Percentage)

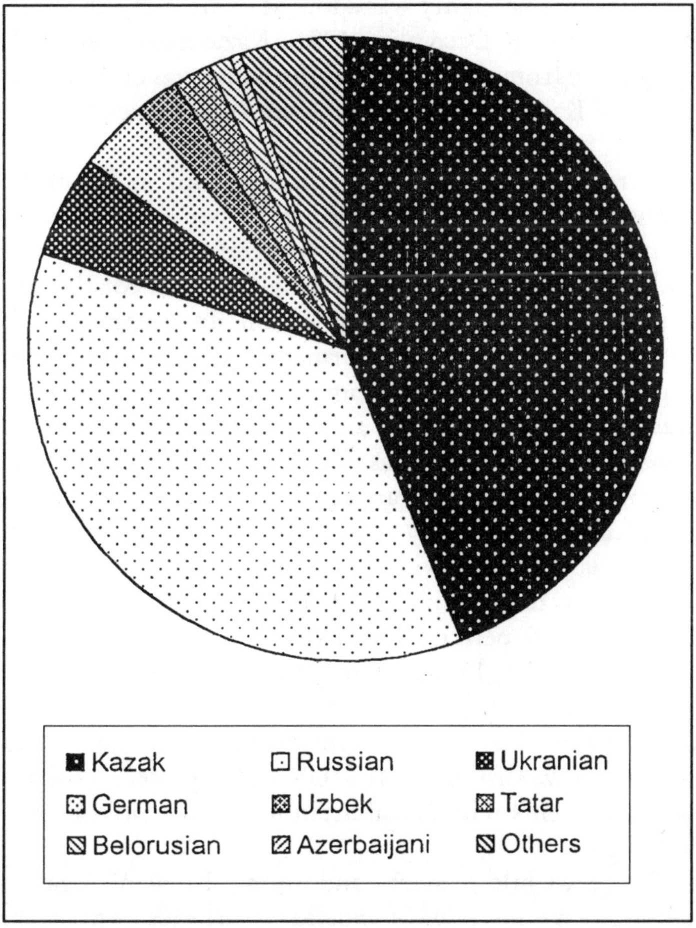

When Kazakhstan came under Russian occupation, many Russian and Ukranian peasants moved to Kazakhstan. However, the immigration led to disaffection with Russian rule, and in 1916, a major rebellion against Russian rule was brutally suppressed killing 1,50,000 people.

It was in 1936, that the Kazakh, Autonomous Soviet Socialist Republic (ASSR) was formed. On 25 October 1990, a declaration of Sovereignty was adopted by the Kazakh Supreme Soviet and on 16 December 1991, Kazakhstan declared its independence from the USSR and the name was changed to the Republic of Kazakhstan and Nursultan Nazarbayev became its President.

There is a multiplicity of ethnic groups in Kazakhstan. The Russian community constitutes 38 per cent of the total population while ethnic Kazakh comprise 40 per cent. In 1993 Kazakh was indicated as the state language with Russian as the language of inter-states communication. In subsequent years there was mass emigration of Germans, Russians and large scale immigration or Kazakh from Mongolia, Turkmenistan, Tajikistan and Kyrgyzstan, and the percentage of Kazakh population in recent years has increased to 53 per cent. Among the major ethnic minorities are the Russians and the Ukrainians (Table 6 and Figure 7).

Islam is the most widespread religion, but secularism is guaranteed by the constitution. The composition of the new Kazakhstan is 59 per cent: Kazakh, 28 per cent, Russian and other nationalities 13 per cent. Nursultan Nazarbayev has preserved racial harmony and has firmly established democratic principles and this has won international recognition and respect for Kazakhstan. Several US and European companies signed agreements with Kazakhstan to explore petroleum and gas reserves.

The erstwhile Soviet and now Russian legacy to Kazakhstan is the pile of nuclear warheads which make Kazakhstan as the fourth largest nuclear power in the world. It was in late 1991 that USSR was dissolved, but Kazakhstan declared its commitment as a non-nuclear free state, by destroying the nuclear weapons or transferring them to the Russian Federation.

The maximum density of population is found in the state of Uzbekistan (46.4 per sq km) and is followed by Tajikistan

(38.2), Kyrgyzstan (22.5), Turkmenistan (8.7) and Kazakhstan (6.2).

Table 5

Kyrgyzstan: Principal Ethnic Groups (1989 Census)

(in percentage)

Kyrgys	52.4
Russian	21.5
Uzbek	12.9
Ukrainian	2.5
German	2.4
Tatar	1.6
Kazak	0.9
Dungan	0.9
Ukagir	0.9
Tajik	0.8
others	3.2

Table 6

Kazakhstan: Principal Ethnic Groups (1994 Census)

(in percentage)

Kazakh	44.3
Russia	35.8
Ukranian	5.1
German	3.6
Uzbek	2.2
Tatar	2.0
Belorusian	1.1
Azerbaijani	0.6
Others	5.3

The five Central Asian states have a combined area of about 4 million sq km (3.99 million sq km) (1.542 million sq miles) with a total population of 58.3 million (2004), and the projected population in 2020 is estimated at 74.69 million. The state which has the largest area in Central Asia is Kazakhstan

(2.7173 million sq km), while the smallest state is Tajikistan with an area of 0.4474 million sq km. The state having the largest population is Uzbekistan, 26.5 million (2004) or 45.4 per cent of the total population of all the states combined (2004) and the state having the least population is Turkmenistan (4,940,000 or 8.64 per cent of the combined population of all states). It will thus be seen that Kazakhstan is the biggest state in area compared to all the others and occupies more than double of the total area of all the four states, while the smallest state is Tajikistan from the viewpoint of area, and the most populous state is Uzbekistan which contains a little less then half the total population of Central Asia (45 per cent) and the least population is in Turkmenistan. The capital towns of the states are Ashgabat (old Ashkhabad) (Turkmenistan), Tashkent (Uzbekistan) Almati (old Alma Ata) (Kazakhstan). Other towns which have been famous the world over are Samarkand, Bukhara and Fergana.

2

Geographic Profile of Central Asian States

The geography of Central Asian region is interesting. It extends from Caspian Sea in the west to the Chinese frontier in the east, bordered by Kazakhstan in the north and Iran and Afghanistan in the south. Parts of the area are marked by extreme aridity like the Karakum and Kyzlkum, the two largest deserts of Central Asia, and these fall in the states of Turkmenistan, Uzbekistan and Kazakhstan.

Central Asian region is marked by two inland seas, the Caspian Sea in the west and the Aral Sea in the centre-west. Caspian Sea is the largest inland lake of the world. Its area is 163,825 sq miles (424,305 sq km). The sea bottom seems to be subsiding as the sea level has been gradually falling since 1929. The reason of falling sea level is the reduction in the discharge of rivers.

The Aral Sea, lying to the east of Caspian Sea, partly falls in Kazakhstan and partly in Uzbekistan. It is the fourth largest inland lake of the world with an area of 24,635 sq miles (63,804

Central Asia: Physical Features

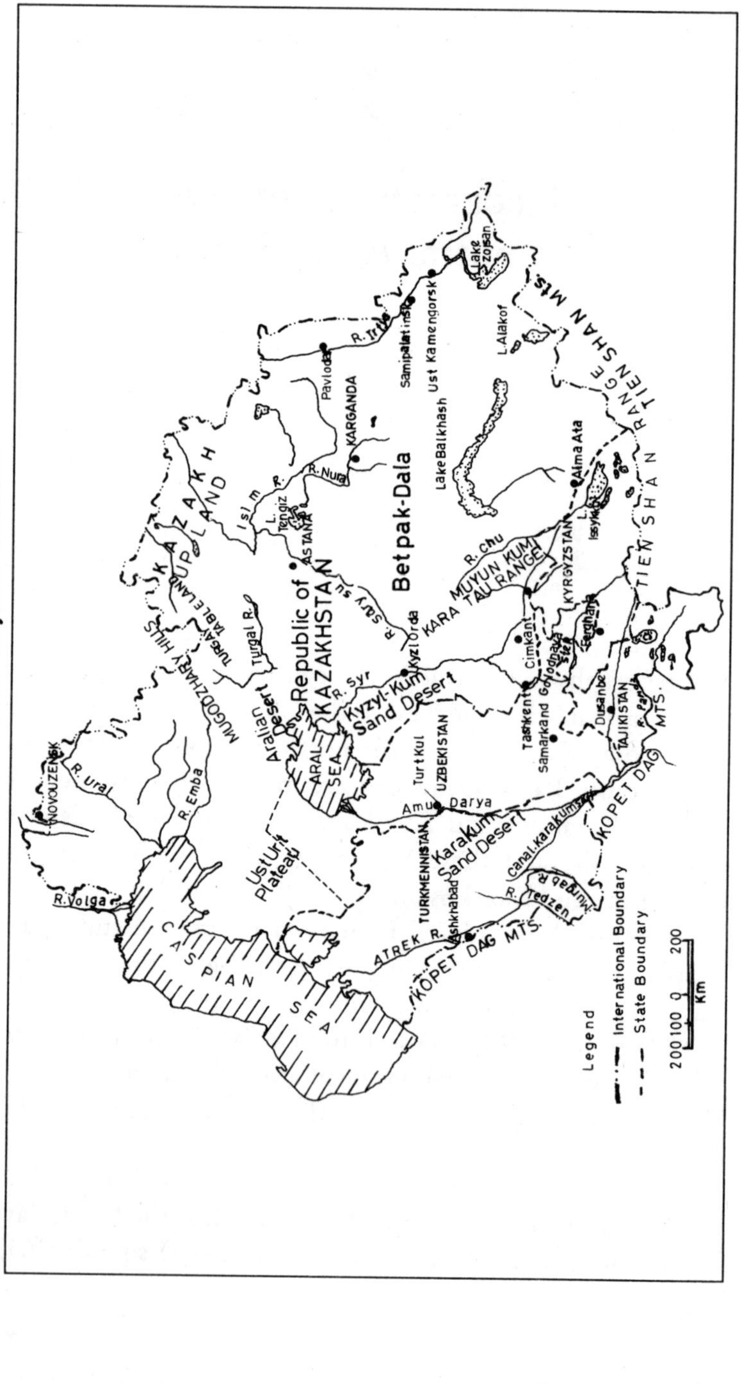

sq km). Its average depth varies between 10 and 20 metres with a maximum depth of 75 metres along the western shore.

Central Asian states can be said to be the gift of two rivers Syr Darya and Amu Darya which fall into the Aral Sea. But, for these rivers, the states of Turkmenistan, Uzbekistan and Kazakhstan would have been a total desert.

Amu Darya is the bigger and more important than Syr Darya. It is fed by the glacier of the Pamir-Alay mountain system. The river is formed by the confluence of two rivers, the Panj and the Vakhsh. It is a swift flowing stream, and descending from the mountain it turns north-west into the desert region and falls into the Aral Sea, making a wide delta. Owing to its high speed and variability of its course, it is not very suitable for irrigation. The Syr Darya rises from the Tein Shan mountain. As compared to Amu Darya, it is smaller in volume, width and depth, but it is greater in length than Amu Darya and much less swift compared to Amu Darya. Syr Darya is very suitable for irrigation.

Although irrigation has turned large areas of the desert in Uzbekistan and Tajikistan into productive lands, it has caused ecological disaster. Today, about 7 million hectares in the Aral region are irrigated, with annual withdrawal of 60 cubic km of water from the Amu Darya and 45 cubic km from Syr Darya. By 1990 the sea level of Aral Sea fell by 14 metres compared to 1960 level and its volume decreased by more than 60 per cent.[1]

The Central Asia region is marked by sandy deserts in the north, while the eastern section covered by the states of Tajikistan and Kyrgyzstan are mostly mountainous, where Tien Shan mountain is most extensive and prominent. It consists of a number of ranges running east to west and on some of them perpetual patches of snow can be seen. The mountain belongs to the Hercynian system. There are extensive valleys in between the ranges which rising to 8,200 metres is the highest peak in central Asia and here lies one of the greatest glaciers of the world, the Feddchenko glacier. Near the Iranian border, in the south, lies a small range: Kopet Dag while Balkan range lies near the Caspian Sea.

Mention should be made of lakes in the mountains: the Issyk Kul with an area of 6,203 sq km (2,395 sq miles) at a height of 18,000 metres. The lake does not freeze in winter. In the Pamir plateau there are two lakes: Kara Kul and Zor Kul.

It will thus be seen that the following physiographic divisions can be identified in the Central Asian lands.

Eastern Sand Ridge Deserts and Uplands

It is low sandy desert punctuated by irrigated oases. This low land stretching from Caspian Sea to Syr Darya contains Central Asia's two largest deserts – the Kara Kum and the Kyzyl Kum. The deserts are separated by Amu River. Kara Kum is predominantly a sandy desert punctuated by dry river beds. In the south of the Kara Kum, along the Iranian frontier lies a narrow belt of oases.

The Kyzyl Kum is a rocky desert and stands higher than the Kara Kum desert. In the eastern parts of this rocky plateau there are long depressions or valleys covered by grasses like the Fergana valley which is densely populated.

It is a very dry desert and it is only along the margins where some water is obtained from the Syr or Amu Darya that cultivation is possible.

The Caspian Basin Region

In the north and east of the Caspian Sea, there lies the old Caspian lake bed where many salt lakes exist. The rivers, Ural and Emba, drain through the flat land below sea level into the Caspian. The area between the two rivers is marked by oil fields. It is near the peninsula Mangyshlak which projects into the Caspian, that the depressed land comes to an end. This area is also known for its oil, manganese and phosphates.

Further south lies the Gulf Kara-Bogaz-Gol. The Gulf is about 35 metres below sea level. The Gulf is cut off from the Caspian Sea by sandbars and the connecting passage is 200 metres wide and about 3 metres deep, while the average depth of the Gulf is 10 metres and its surface level often falls by about 4 metres below the level of the Caspian, with huge annual evaporation. This raises the salt content of the Gulf. It has been calculated that between 10 and 20 cubic kilometres of water are evaporated from Kara-Bogaz-Gol annually and the salt content is very high. It may be noted that the entire coast of the Caspian from the northern end, southward all along the eastern side is a desert and barren. South of the Kara-Bogaz-Gol is a plateau to the south-east of which there are several ranges called Balkan Ranges.

In the northern part of the Caspian Sea, two rivers, Ural from the Ural Mountain and the Emba from the north-east coming from the Mugodzhar Mountain, flow into the Caspian. The importance lies in the oil bearing areas of Emba fields in the north, the Mangyshalak fields in the centre and Nebit Dag in the south. There are small fishing towns on the coast with acute water supply problem.

It is interesting to note that there is such an acute shortage of water that the biggest port on the Caspian; Turkmeenbashi (old: Krasnovodsk) gets its drinking water by tankers across the Caspian from the Kura River in Transcaucasia. Of late, desilting pilot plants have been installed and the desalination process produces much cheaper drinking water than fresh water obtained from tankers.

The Ust-Yurt Plateau is barren upland and lies between Caspian and the Aral Sea with an elevation of 300 metres. The lack of water makes it a desert area.

The Turarian Lowland

East of the Ust Yurt plateau lies the plain region known as Turanian lowland. In its middle portion lies the Aral Sea, which is the fourth largest lake in the world, with a surface area of about 64.7 million sq m (25,000 sq miles). Its depth is between 10 and 20 metres. It is a shallow sea and contains thousands of islands. Aral Sea means inland sea. In the north-east the Syr Darya has built a delta into the lake, while in the south lies the delta of the Amu Darya. In the past the Aral Sea was connected with the Caspian. The two big rivers draining into the Aral Sea have brought down its salinity to 1 per cent while that of Caspian Sea is 14.

The Turarian lowland is much more rocky compared to Kara Kum. It rises to an elevation of 1,000 metres in the central and south-western portion. It is a very dry desert and it is only along the margins where some water is obtained from the Syr or Amu Darya and cultivation becomes possible.

To the north-east of the Syr Darya is the Kaya Tau or Black Mountain. Further east lies Muyun Kum or sandy desert. There are two rivers which border Muyum Kum or sandy desert, Talass in the west and the Chu in the east. These rivers rise from the Tien Shan in the south and flow northward and are lost in the sand. However, the Chu Valley is the dividing line between Muyun Kum and Betpak Dala.

Betpak Dala literally means cruel, crafty and clever steppe. It is so called because, having no tracks, on hot days, it presents pictures of mirages and travellers are deceived. The elevation of this dry plateau rises from 50 metres in the south to 500 metres in the north. The Betpak Dala is also called the Hungry Steppe. The vegetation is very sparse and development is difficult as the topography is highly uneven consisting of cracked clay and salt encrustation.

Betpak Dala (the Hungry Steppe) should not be mixed up with the less extensive Hungry Steppe in the south-west of Tashkent where with the help of irrigation, cotton is extensively cultivated and the area is called Cotton Island.

A prominent feature in the landscape is Lake Balkhash which should not escape attention. This lake is 560 km (350 miles) long and lies at a height of about 400 metres above sea level. Its total area is about 17,300 sq km (6,680 sq miles) with an average depth of 7 metres. It is believed that the lake at one time extended further to east, and the water in the lake is of recent geological origin as its salt content is low. At the western end it receives water from the Ili river, and the water is fit for irrigation and drinking purposes. There is a sandbar in the middle of the lake and divides the lake into two parts. The western part where the water is relatively fresh and the eastern part, owing to evaporation the water has a high salt content.

High Mountains

Central Asia is bounded in the west, south and east by high rugged mountains.

In the west, bordering on Iran lies Kopet Dag or Dry Mountain. It is about 2,500 metres high and it is so dry that even the highest parts are devoid of vegetation.

East of Kopet Dag lies the Hindu Kush Mountain. They wholly lie in Afghanistan. Their main significance is that small streams taking their rise from the mountain flow northward into Central Asia and of these two large streams are the Murgab and the Tedzhen rivers. These streams which end in the sands of Turkmenistan are the basis of two oases round the cities of Mary and Tedzhen.

The Hindu Kush in eastern Afghanistan joins the Pamir Knot which skirts the boundaries of Afghanistan, Pakistan and China. On the extreme east, the ranges are called Pamir Aley with peaks ranging between 8,000 and 9,000 metres and lie in the Tajik Republic called Tien Shan mountain.

It is an extensive mountain system which means a heavenly mountain (Chinese term). It covers northern Tajikistan and passing through Uzbekistan and Kyrgyzstan, and through Kazakhstan, east of Lake Balkhash it passes into China. The ranges run from west to east and enclose mountain basins, the broadest being Fergana Basin. It is an alluvial basin about 160 km east-west and 16 to 40 km wide. It is the major agricultural area of Central Asia.

Tien Shan is of great economic importance to Central Asia. There are many flourishing irrigated areas and cities at their base. The ranges enclose many smaller lakes. Their importance further lies in the fact that the Syr Darya rises along the southern slope of the ranges and flowing through Feragana Basin enters the desert to the north-west. The river is fed by melting of glaciers and is flooded during summers when water is most needed. Most of the snowfall comes in winter months.

Thus, the mountainous portions with snow patches harbour glaciers from which the two rivers Syr and Amu Darya flow. The Tien Shah Mountain system is the main mountain of Central Asia. It is quite extensive. It consists of several ranges. On the tertiary mountain south of Tien Shah lies one of the greatest glacier of the world: Fedehenco glacier about 80 km long.

Climate

The climate of Central Asia is continental, hot in the summer and cold in winters. The average temperature in the summers in the lowlands may rises to 40°C while in winters it may go a few degrees below freezing. The precipitation is very scanty and ranges from 10 to 12 cm per annum, while it increases in the foothills and averages between 40 and 45 cm. The summers are long, hot and dry. Dry winds blowing from the north, raise sandstorms in the desert. Sometimes, the dust storms are so fierce that visibility is reduced to zero and the sky is covered with a ball of dust. Summers in the lowland are so intense that all work must be suspended during the hottest hours; activity out of doors is impossible as long as the sun is above the horizon. The air is very dry and humidity sometimes goes down to as low as 1 per cent. Winters are equally severe. The Amu begins to freeze in the beginning of September, and is snow bound by the end of October.

The extremes of temperatures are particularly marked in the mountainous regions and in the Pamirs, but in the valleys the climate is relatively cold. In the Fergana Valley the climate is pleasant. December, January and February are very cold months and snowfall is common particularly in the mountain region, but with the onset of the month of March, the temperature changes suddenly. From March to August, the season is warm to hot. May, June, July and August are particularly hot months: towards the end of August or beginning of September summer becomes mild and is followed by a warm autumn. The months of September and October are the most pleasant months in Central Asia. The contrast in temperature in the mountainous areas and the plains is significant. Frosts are common even in July in the Pamirs and in winters the temperature may fall much below the freezing point (–20°C).

Vegetation

Steppe vegetation covers the plains as well as the mountain slopes. The trees are scattered and have stunted growth. In the desert the dominant tree is Saxaul (Holoxylon) a knotted twisted leafless tree which grows to a height of 7 metres with a trunk diameter of 35 cm (Plate 1). Extravagant grazing has destroyed the vegetation in many places in the desert, providing a free mobility of sand dunes in the desert, but wherever vegetation is intact, the dunes are immobile. Along the rivers and lakes a grass is found which is called *Chiy*, which often reaches a height of 4 metres and is used by the local population for making mats and for thatching roofs.

On the lower slopes of the mountains, deciduous forest are common and the typical trees are Walnut, Pistachio, and Apricot: Pine and Oak trees are generally absent. Higher up in the mountains the forests are replaced by rich pastures like the Alpine meadows.

Irrigation and Environmental Hazards

The maximum irrigation is to be found in the Aral Sea basin, which is drained by the rivers Amu and the Syr. As a result of heavy irrigation development, the Aral Sea has been shrinking over the last 40 years. The areas of the Aral Sea in the 1950s was 66,000 sq km with a mean depth of 16 metres. The desert basin has been transformed into smiling fields. About 7 million hectares of land in Aral region are irrigated. This has resulted in

Plate 1
Saxaul Trees

the sharp decline of inflow of water in the Aral and the sea level came down from 53 metres in 1960 to 39 metres in 1989. The area of the sea has shrunk by more than 40 per cent and its volume has decreased by more than 60 per cent. As a result the ecological balance in this region has been worsened. The Aral Sea has lost its productive fisheries and by 2000 AD, the salinity of the sea rose to almost 4 per cent. The exposed sea bottom of the Aral is becoming a salty bad land. Dust storms have become common in spring and the sulphates and chlorides are harmful to desert oases and pastures. The polluted drain water from the irrigated fields returns to the river and lowers the water quality.

From the ecological hazard of the basin, it has led to human health hazards. The use of chemical toxic water has affected the health of the people.

Irrigation is a mixed blessing. In a region where there is little rainfall, nothing can be grown without the help of irrigation. In the loess-covered foothills in the south, where precipitation averages between 25 and 40 cm per annum, in the winter and early summer months, crops like wheat can be grown without irrigation, but in the Central Asian region, as a whole, rainfall is very scanty and water becomes the life-blood of Central Asia. The major difficulty in canal irrigation is that there is excessive use of water. In a region where the soil is largely sandy, water percolates in the sub-soil with dissolved salt and by capillary action again comes to the surface making the soil more saline. However, many irrigation projects have been undertaken from the ancient times. These ancient constructions were made on the smaller streams or at the lower portions of the bigger streams where it was easier to make the dams. The lack of technology prevented them to harness the large rivers where they issued forth from the mountains. In modern times, large dams have been constructed in the gorges where the major rivers, the Amu Darya and the Syr Darya, leave the mountains and enter the plains. Figure 8 shows the major irrigated areas of Central Asia.

Figure 8
Irrigation: Central Asia

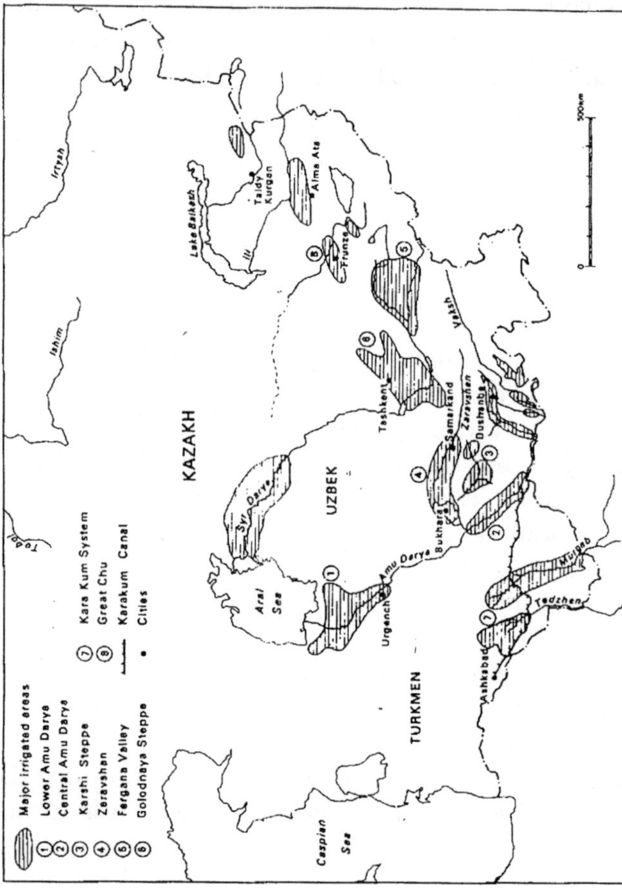

Source: Symons, L. et al., (1983), *The Soviet Union: A Systematic Geography*, Bangalore, p. 77.

The Great Fergana Canal

This canal was completed in 1939. Before the construction of this canal, only the southern portion of the Fergana basin was irrigated from minor streams. There are numerous small streams which flow down the northern slope of the Alay Range and with gravity flow-irrigation, the southern part of the basin was irrigated. The Fergana Canal utilizes the waters of the Syr Darya which flows for full length of the basin. The main canal is about 320 km long and completely encircles the Fergana Basin. There are many distributary canals which distribute the water over the basin and to-day over a million hectares are irrigated. The Namangan irrigation canal was completed parallel to the older Great Fergana Canal and this canal provides irrigation water to over 30,000 hectares.

Farkhand Dam

At the western end of the Fegana Basin where the Syr Drya gushes out through a gorge on its way to the Hungry Steppe in the west, a dam has been built called Farkhand Dam. This dam provides water for irrigation to expand cultivation in the cotton island (Prkhta Aral) in the Hungry Steppe. It also provides hydroelectricity to the chemical and synthetic industries.

Kayrak Kum (Friendship of Nations) Dam

This dam has been built on the Syr Darya at the western end of the Fergana Basin. This reservoir is known as Tajik Sea, 70 km long within the neck of Tajikistan and completed in 1957. It feeds 12 networks of irrigation canals and irrigates about half a million hectares of arid land of which 0.3 million hectares lie in the Hungry Steppes in the Uzbeck Republic and also irrigates some land in northern Tajikistan. This is multi-purpose project, and the hydroelectric plant has a capacity of 0.15 million kilowatts of electricity.

Kokand: Hydroelectric-cum-Irrigation Project

The Kokand project collects water from all the channels of the Sokh river in the south-central part of Fergana basin and provides irrigation to about 70,000 hectares of land and also generates hydroelectricity. As it is constructed at the head of large alluvial fan, it checks the huge sand from passing into the canals both on the right and left of the dam and saves the canals from being choked.

Kara Kum Canal

It is the largest irrigation project of Central Asia. It takes its water from Amu-Darya at Kelif and carries water to the oases of Mary, Tedzehen and Ashgabat (Askhabad) and thus provides irrigation water to the whole of thirsty southern Turkmenistan. The canal was completed in 1962. This canal is a marvel of engineering as the canal, 650 km long, in a region of shifting sands, has been completed in the face of hazard of sandstorms which very often destroyed the work already completed.

One great problem which the construction of the canal faced was the clogging of silt in the canal carried by the Amu Darya. The Amu Darya carries 250 million cubic metres of silt and sand per year, and 8 million cubic metres enter the canal. The canal has been divided with the help of a barrage into three branches. About 6 million cubic metre of sediments are prevented entry into the branches, but 2 cubic million metre sediments sneak through in these branches. There are seventeen excavating pumps which continually remove these sediments and whatever still remains, settles in the Kelif lake which itself is a series of 8 stagnant lakes connected by shallow channels. The lakes are overgrown with water plants, which pose a serious problem to the canal. Tractors pull weeds from the bed of the canal. Moreover, a species of fish is imported from China which feeds on the plants and helps in clearing the canal.

Two-thirds of the Amu Darya water are lost in evaporation and filtration, and only one-third of the water that enters the canal reaches the Murgab Oasis at Mary. In order to provide more water in the canal a large reservoir called Khauz Khan has been built on the Kara Kum canal between the Murgab and Tedzhen rivers so that the canal is kept flowing throughout the year. The winter flow is stored in the reservoir until it is needed for irrigation in summer. Moreover, the reservoir stores the overflow of water from the Tedzehen river, and the excess flow during spring into the Kauzkhan reservoir, is used for irrigation. The Khauz Khan reservoir was completed in the seventies with a capacity of 1.3 billion cubic metres of water.

Other Minor Projects

1. *Amu Karakul Canal*: It which starts from Chardzhou upto 54 km in a north-easterly direction across the Kyzyl Kum desert to the Karakul Oasis at the end of Zeravshan river. The project was completed in three years. This canal brings water to the lower Zeravashan river. Zeravshan is a small river and does not have enough water to irrigate the rich fertile land from Samarkand through Bukhara to Karakul.
2. *Amu Bukghara Canal*: This canal is 160 km long. The Amu-Karakul canal after 20 km branches off towards east taking water from the Amu Darya to Kuyu Mazar reservoir to the north-east of Bukhara. The water is pumped to a height of 48 metres and through gravity flow the water goes into distributaries. The canal in its different phases of construction irrigates about 0.3 million hectares of cotton land.
3. *Amu Darya Karshi Canal*: The canal lies in south-eastern Uzbekistan. Water from Amu Darya is pumped to a height of 150 metres to a reservoir from which water is brought by gravity flow to the canal which provides irrigation to Kaska basin to the tune of 0.3 million hectares of long staple cotton.

South Surkhan Project

Surkhan Darya basin is in the extreme south of Uzbekistan near the Kaekha Darya basin. An earthen Dam with a height of 32 metres has been built across the Surkhan Darya which provides irrigation to about 0.2 million hectares of land in the valley where the Surkhan river joins Amu Darya at Termez. The climate is very favourable for the growth of cotton as the season is completely frost-free and promotes high yield of cotton.

The Vakhsh Basin

Vakhsh is a tributary, which join Amu Darya from north-east and irrigate lands in the south-west of Tajikistan and makes possible the cultivation of long staple cotton. To the south-east of Dushanbe a high dam known as Nurek Dam has been built on the Vakhsh. The dam is one km long and 300 metres high. This is a multi-purpose project and besides providing irrigation facilities it has hydroelectric capacity of about 3 million kilowatts.

It will be seen that what was formerly barren land is now converted into fertile fields with intensive production of cotton (generally without crop rotation) and having large plantation of rice. The development is at the cost of environment. Central Asia must decide whether the current use of excessive water should be continued and in the long run replace the Aral Sea by a 60,000 sq km salt and sand desert. If the excessive use of water is continued, it would be an environmental disaster. Naturally, the position should not be acceptable, hence the pattern of cropping should be changed: rice should be replaced by crops that need much less water, like millet. Cotton, as a monoculture, should be accompanied by crop rotation, and irrigation should be planned with proper drainage facilities.

Agriculture

The predominant occupation of people in Central Asia is agriculture, while livestock raising and herding come next in importance. Irrigated farming has led to intensive cultivation of cotton, alfalfa, vegetables and fruits as well as rice, but where agriculture depends on rainfall, dry farming of grain in the moister portions of loess covered foothills of the southern mountains is carried on. In the dry lowlands and in the high mountains where cultivation is not possible, the whole of the lowland from the Caspian Sea to the eastern end of lake Balkhash and extending to the southern border of Turkmenistan no cultivation is possible, except for scattered regions of irrigation. Even grazing is poor throughout the drier areas, while in many areas grazing is limited to spring and early summer after the melting of snow which produces an abundance of ephemeral vegetation [2] (Figure 9 shows

Figure 9

Central Asia: Agricultural Regions

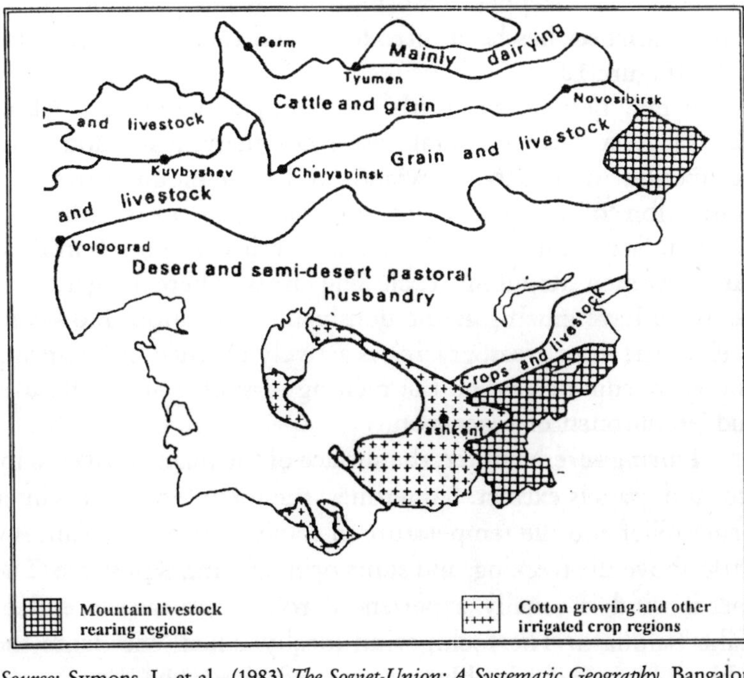

Source: Symons, L. et al., (1983) *The Soviet-Union: A Systematic Geography*, Bangalore, p. 120.

agricultural regions and Figure 10 shows cultivated lands in Central Asia).

Cotton on irrigated lands is the predominant crop. The warm and sunny climate of Central Asia and the fertile soil of the valley together with irrigation have promoted the cultivation of cotton. Fergana Valley, the oases of Tashkent, Samarkand, Bukhara and Vakhsh Valley are the chief centres of cotton production. The seeds are crushed for oil and the refuse is used as food for animals (Figure 9). Other cereal crops grown in Central Asia are rice, wheat, corn and sesame. Central Asia is also known for its orchards. Apricots, peaches, apples, grapes, pears, pomegranates are widely grown along with a variety of vegetables. Dried fruits particularly raisins are exported. In the high mountain valleys in summer, livestock grazing is common while in the winters the people with their livestock come down to the lowland steppes. Transhumance is practised on a large scale. Sugarbeet has been introduced and tobacco is also cultivated (Figure 10).

It may be pointed out that though grazing of livestock in Central Asia is carried on almost everywhere; it is a dominant occupation in the drier lowlands and high mountains where cultivation of cereals is not possible. The areas from the Caspian Sea to the end of Balkhash and the southern border of the Turkmen Republic, excluding areas where irrigation is possible, have grazing as the dominant occupation. However, even in the drier areas, grazing is actively pursued in the spring and early summer, when the melting of snows brings about a sudden outburst of vegetation.

During severe winter, the surface of the plain is covered by ice, and grass is extinct. Sometimes, the foehn winds in winter bring relief and the temperature in some parts of the plain is a little above the freezing, and some open grazing is possible. The foehn wind is usually experienced round the eastern end of Lake Balkhash. The foehn wind locally called ‘ebe’ from the Sikiang basin in China blows westwards down the slope.

Figure 10

Central Asia: Cultivated Land

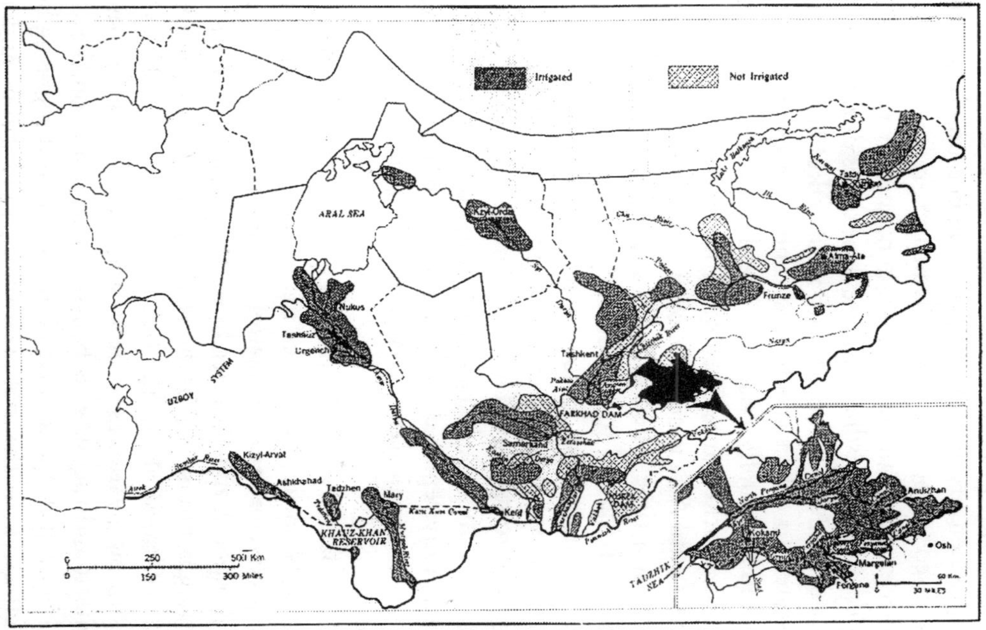

Source: Lydolph, Paul E., (1969), *Geography of The U.S.S.R.*, New York, p. 244.

It may be pointed out that the major problem of the extensive deserts of Central Asia is stabilization of sand dunes and realization in this respect is gradually coming in. The wandering of the herdsmen has been considerably reduced, and the herdsmen are placing greater reliance on forage and hay crops raised in rotation with cotton and grain.

For example alfalfa is grown in rotation with cotton in the irrigated areas and is harvested several times during the year.

Central Asia is famous for its Karakul sheep, which are well suited to desert conditions. These are curly haired black sheep and are chiefly raised for the skin of the newborn lambs and in the world market they bring high prices. Their main area in the Central Asia is near the oasis of Zeravshan river (Plate 2). There was a time when camel was the main beast of burden, being highly suited to the desert condition. The 'Silk Road' between China and Europe passed through Tashkent and Samarkand and camels were the main means of transport along the caravan route, but of late their importance has declined and sheep and camel are important sources of meat and they have been generally replaced by the donkey as beast of burden and in the cities mechanical means of transport with facilities of oil are common.

The sparse vegetation does help in the stabilization of sand dunes, but mention should be made of a species of stunted tree very effective in the stabilization of sand in Central Asia. It is a rugged, knotty and weather beaten tree which is about 6 to 7 metres high and is very hard. This stunted tree is a boon to the desert of Central Asia. The tree is called *Saxaul* (Plate 1). This tree is of two varieties: One is white and grows on the sand dune itself and the other is black, which grows on the alkaline lands between the sand dunes. It does not need watering but it is very effective in the stabilization of sand dunes and it also provides fuel to the poor people. Earlier, the wood of this tree had been extensively used by the herdsmen as fuel, as the desert region permits the cold Siberian wind to come straight up to Tashkant in the absence of any obstruction, and the

Plate 2
Drying Karakul Skins

temperature usually goes below freezing during the winter. The herdsmen in their makeshift camp shiver without fire; hence there was a large scale use of the wood of this tree. The utility of this tree has dawned upon the people as an effective and powerful stabilizing agent for the drifting sands when it began to be extinct from certain areas owing to large scale cutting for fuel purposes.

Minerals

Central Asia is rich in minerals, but it is only in recent years that scientific geological exploration has been started. There are extensive deposits of crude oil and gas. The main oilfields for a long time had been Emba along the northern shore of the Caspian and the field lying in the vicinity of Nebit Dog south of Kara-Bogaz-Gol in the Turkmenistan Republic. However, in the sixties, as a result of exploration, new fields at Zhetybay in the southern part of Mangyshlak Peninsula in Kazakhstan and at Uzen further north-east was discovered (Figure 11). By 1970, crude oil output on Magyshlak was about 15 million tonnes and the total production in Kazakhstan rose to 23 million tonnes in 1993.

Another potential areas of oil production in Central Asia is Turkmenistan. The main producing fields are in Nebit Dog and production has increased in recent years and in 1992 the total production was about 5 million tonnes and Uzbekistan produced 4 million tonnes of crude oil.

Gas

Turkmenistan's annual production of gas in 1992 was 30 million cubic metres and in 1993 the production of gas in Uzbekistan was 45 million cubic metres. Figure 11 shows the oil and gas fields of Central Asia.

Coal and Ferrous Metal

Central Asia is not rich in coal deposits. There are small coal deposits in the Fergana Basin and the surrounding mountains.

Figure 11

Central Asia: (Oilfields and Gas Fields)

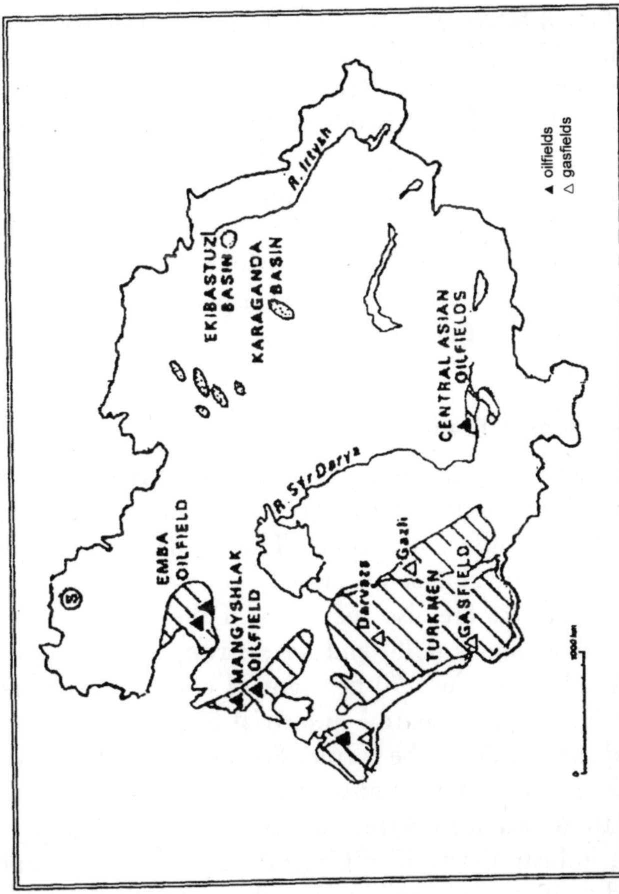

Source: Symons, L. et al., (1983), *The Soviet Union: A Systematic Geography.*

In the Fergana Basin, coal comes from the western part of the basin. Another important deposit of coal lies in the Karaganda fields in northern Kazakhstan. Central Asia is also poor in respect of iron ore. There are low grade iron ore deposits in the Turgay lowland north of Aral Sea. However, with the supply of coal from Karaganda field an iron and steel industry has been established. Central Asia is rich in non-ferrous metals. Rich deposits of copper in Central Asia occur at Balkhash on the northern shore of Lake Balkhash. There is also a minor deposit in the Tien Shan, south-east of Tashkent. Besides, there are deposits of lead, zinc, molybdenum and tungsten.

There are also important deposits of non-metallic minerals, like deposits of mineral salts, phosphate, sulphur, and sodium chloride is obtained from Caspian Sea, the Aral Sea and Lake Balkhash. Figure 12 shows the mineral resources of Central Asia.

Transport and Trade

Water transport is not important in Central Asia as the streams are unsuitable for navigation. They are shallow with fluctuating levels during different seasons. The burden of transport has therefore fallen almost exclusively on railroad. The Central Asian Republics are also members of the Commonwealth of Independent States (CIS) and have strong trade relation with Russia. They produce 90 per cent of cotton of the erstwhile Soviet Union; the Central Industrial Region produces 70 per cent of the textile of the former Soviet Union. In view of this fact, to a large extent, cotton has to be transported to some three thousand kilometres to the industrial region of CIS. Again, industrialization of Central Asia states in recent times has led to heavy movement of coal and petroleum within the Central Asian region.

Population

The total population of Central Asian states (2004) was 58.3 million while in mid-2006 it was 58.6 million as reported by

Figure 12

Central Asia: The Physical Landscape and Mineral Resources

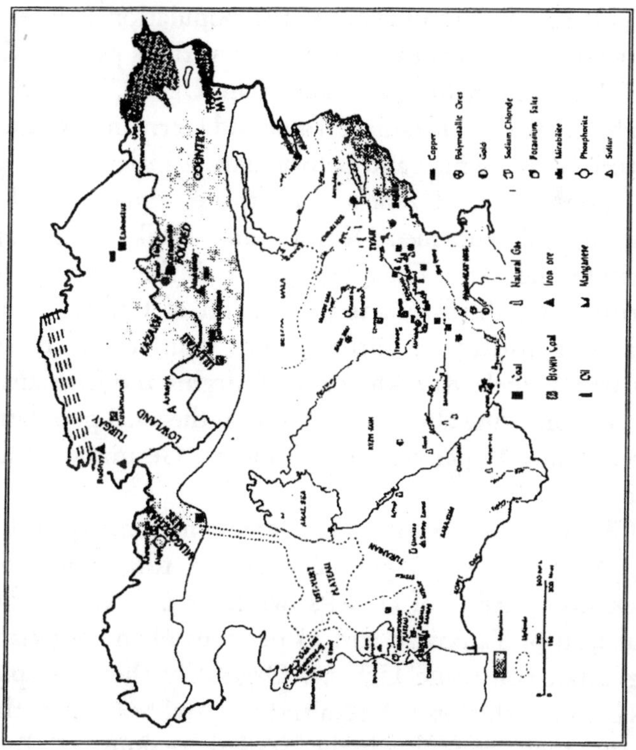

Source: Lydolph Paue E, (1969), *Geography of the USSR*, New York, p. 232.

ESCAP data sheet with an area of 3,994,400 sq km. The average density of population per sq km is 14.6 and in mid-2006 it was 14.7. However, there is a great variation from west to east as well as from north to south. In the extreme west in Turkmenistan the density of population is 8.5 while in Kazakhstan it is 6.3. The maximum density is found in Uzbekistan 52.1.

The ethnic composition of the population is interesting. Persons of 12 nationalities inhabit the various parts of Central Asia. These nationalities are: Turkman, Uzbek, Kazakh, Tajik, Khirghis, Russian, Ukranian, Tatar and German. The numbers of Azerians, Armenian and Belorussians is insignificant. Of the total population, Uzebeks constitute one-third; Kazakh one-sixth and Turkmen, Khirgis and Tajik taken together constitute one-sixth. Thus, persons of all the five nationalities constitute two-thirds of the population of Central Asia. The Russians constitute a little more than one-sixth. Thus, Turkman, Uzbek, Kazakh, Tajik, Khirghis and Russians taken together constitute about 85 per cent of the total population. In the remaining 15 per cent are Ukranins, Germans, Tatars and others.

The Uzbeks constitute the largest nationality in Central Asia. As much as 70 per cent of the total population of Uzbekistan consists of Uzbeks, while 24 per cent of the total population of Tajikistan and 13 per cent of the population of Kyrgyzstan constitute Uzbeks. Originally they occupied the areas between the lower Volga and the Aral Sea, but in the 16th century they conquered the settled regions of Bukhara, Samarkand and Tashkent.

More than 40 per cent (about 7,500,000) Kazakhs live in Kazakhstan. Of them, there are some 800,000 in Uzbekistan and about 900,000 in Turkmenistan. The Kazakhs derive the meaning of their name Kazakh from "riders of the steppes". Earlier, they were nomads but later they got settled down on collective farms. About a million Kazkhs live on the Chinese side of border of Kazakhstan.

Today, Turkmen are confined in Turkmenistan and are more than three million or about three-fourths of the total population of Turkmenistan.

The Tajiks constitute one of the oldest ethnic elements in Central Asia. They constitute about four million in Central Asia, out of which about three million are to be found in Tajikistan and one million in Uzbekistan. The Tajiks constitute about 8 per cent of the total population of Central Asia.

The Khirigis, before the 9th century AD lived in the upper reaches of the Yenesi river and migrated from there to the east of Tienshan. Today, there are two and a half million Khirigis who live in Kyrgyzstan and constitute half the total population of Kyrghzstan and about 5 per cent of the total population of Central Asia.

Central Asia's population is very unevenly distributed. The concentration of population is found in Oases where the soil is fertile and the availability of water makes possible the growing of crops. The mining of mineral resources has also attracted concentration of population.

Notes

1. Kotlyakov. V.M. (1991), "The Aral Sea Basin: A Critical Environmental Zone", *Environment*, Volume 33, Number 1, Washington D.C., M. 5-6.
2. Lydolph Paul, E. (1964), *Geography of the USSR*, New York, p. 240.

3

Turkmenistan

Historical Background

Turkmenistan attained the status of an independent republic on 27 October, 1991, with a new state emblem, flag and national anthem. General Niyazov became the President of the state and also the Head of the government through a general referendum for a period of five years, up to 2002. In December 1998, by an amendment to the constitution, Niyazove's mandate was extended indefinitely. However, in August 2003, Niyazove announced that he would retire in 2007, later on he said that he would not retire before 2010.

Turkmenistan was a part of the erstwhile Soviet Union since 1918. There were minor aberrations but in October 1924, it was declared a part of the Soviet Socialist Republic. The major issues in Turkmenistan in the late 1980s were economic, environmental and cultural. There was strong criticism that Turkmenistan was treated as an appendage to All Union Authorities for supplying raw materials (mainly natural gas and cotton) to the developed republic of European USSR. It was in May, 1990 that Turkman language officially became the state language, replacing Russian and on 22, August the Turkmen Supreme Soviet adopted a declaration of sovereignty with its own political and social system. In December 1991, the Communist Party of Turkmenistan changed its name from Democratic Party of Turkmenistan to the Republic of Turkmenistan, and in December 22, 1992, Turkmenistan became a signatory to the Alma Ata declaration to join the Commonwealth of Independent States (CIS). Although the population is predominantly Muslim, Turkmenistan's constitution guarantees state secularism. President Niyazove has strongly emphasized it. In 1992, Turkmenistan entered into a number of agreements relating to political, economic and cultural relations with other countries and also signed an accord to construct a railway line between Iran and Turkmenistan. Turkmenistan and Turkey signed an agreement for the construction of a pipeline to supply natural gas from Turkmenistan to Europe via Iran and Turkey.

Area and Population

Turkmenistan with an area of 488,100 sq km and a population of 4,940,000 in 2004 (according to the ESCAP population data sheet, 2004) lies in the extreme west of the Central Asian states. The density of population is 10.1 per sq km. From the view-point of nationality, 73 per cent of the population is Turkmen. Russians are 10 per cent while the Uzbeks are 9 per cent; the remaining 8 per cent consist of Kazakh, Tatar, Ukrainian, Armenian and Belorusian (Table 2 and Figure 13).

Turkmenistan is bordered on the west by the Caspian Sea, in the north lies the Kazakh Republic, in the east the Amu Darya and the Uzbek Republic, in the south lies Iran and in the south-east is Afghanistan (Figure 13).

Relief

Turkmenistan is the most arid of all the Central Asian states; a large portion of the territory in the north is taken up by the Kara Kum desert. The desert, in fact, occupies about 75 per cent

Figure 13
Turkmenistan

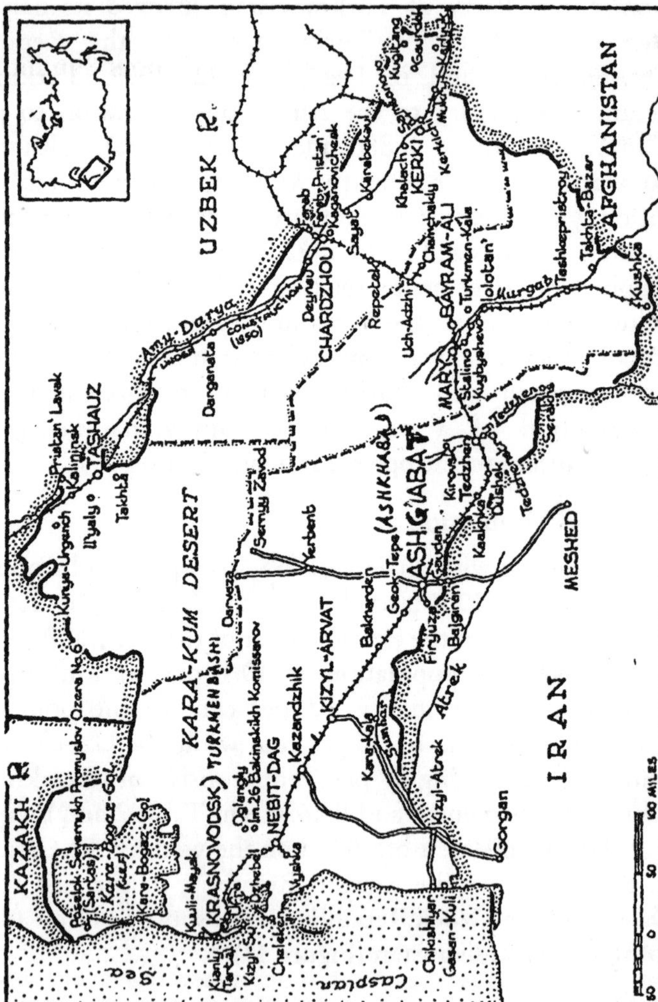

of the republic and is one of the largest deserts of the world. The redeeming features are the oases formed by the streams, which descend from the Kopet Dag and other ranges in the south. These rivers are Murgab and Tedzhen. The oases in the north-east are formed by the Amu Darya. It is a rolling lowland desert, the topography sloping westward towards the Caspian.

Climate

The climate of the republic is continental: hot and dry in summer and cold in winter. The average January temperature in the south is 2°C while in the north it is –4°C. The July temperature varies from 32°C in the south to 30°C in the north. Rainfall is scanty and the average is 10-20 cm a year, received in winters, while on the slopes of mountains it may go upto 40 cm. Thus, scarcity of water and abundance of sunshine are the typical features of Turkmenistan. Turkmenistan is marked by paucity of water.

Vegetation

Vegetation is scarce. The greater parts of the Kara Kum sand desert are covered with a sparse, stiff vegetation which provides fodder to the cattle. Large tracts of the desert-land have been planted and they make immense pastures for the sheep and goats.

Irrigation and Agriculture

Agriculture in Turkmenistan can be practised only with the help of irrigation and covers about 90 per cent of the total sown area. The Kara Kum canal is the lifeline of Turkmenistan. The canal crosses the desert for over 600 km, between the upper Amu Darya at Kelif and Ashgabat. The canal has been completed in two sections. The first section carries Amu Darya water westward and links it with the ancient irrigation system on the Murgab river and Tedzhen river and also the oases of Ashgabat. The reservoir on the Murghab and the Tedzhen rivers and the Kara Kum Canal, which connects the two rivers with Amu Darya near Kelif, is a source of great irrigation. The Kara Kum canal has been extended to the Caspian and the canal irrigates about one million hectares of land.

However, the canal is not without its attendant problems. The major problem is the silting of the canal. It is estimated that about 8 million cubic metres of sediments enter the canal from the Amu Darya each year and the canal is silting up at many points. Sand blown from the desert is another problem, which the canal faces, Tree plantation has been taken up to prevent the blowing sands. The western extension of the canal linking the Amu Darya delta near Nukus with the Caspian Sea near Turkmenbashi (Karasnovodsk) is provided with branch canals and hydroelectric station.

Crops

Cotton is the major crop in the irrigated areas, under the hot sun in the Murgab and the Tedzhen oases and along the Amu Darya. The best varieties of cotton with long silky fibre, are grown. In 2001 it produced 184,000 tonnes of cotton lint. While in 2002, its production was 148,000 metric tonnes. The cultivation of wheat in recent years has been increasing. In 2000 the production was 1,150,000 metric tonnes but in 2001 it rose to 1,760,000 metric tonnes and in 2002 the production was 2,200,000 metric tonnes. Among the food grains, barley is next in importance and contributed 28,000 metric tonnes in 2002. The production of rice was 80,000 tonnes in 2002. Roots and tubers, 30,000 metric tonnes. The cultivation of vegetables, grapes and melons is also important. Turkmenistan boasts of the sweetest grapes and melons in the world. Table 7 shows the production of various crops.

Livestock and Livestock Products

Sheep belonging to the finest breed (the Karakul breed) constitute the herds of Turkmenistan. Horses of very fine breed and camels are also raised. The desert vegetation of Kara Kum supplies the fodder. In summer, the herds of sheep are taken to

Table 7
Principal Crops

(in 000 metric tonnes)

	2000	*2001*	*2002*
Wheat	1150	1760	2200
Rice	27.3	39	80
Barley	22	22.8	28.5
Cabbage	35	32	30
Tomatoes	145	155	150
Dry onion	53	40.9	50
Carrot	32	35.7	35
Other vegetables	31600	39800	31
Watermelon	240	235	230
Grape	140	135	130
Apple	19	18	20
Other Fruits and Berries	27	26	25.5
Cotton Lint	232.6	184	148

Source: Europa, Vol. II, 2004.

the foothills and to the mountain and plateaus in the south, while in the winters the herds are brought back to the low-lands. Efforts have been made to rationalize livestock raising and the Kara Kum has been sufficiently developed to provide fodder for a very large number of herds of livestock. The number of sheep in 2000 was over 5.6 million and in 2001 as well as in 2002 it was 6 million respectively and the number of horses was 17,000 (2002). There were 860,000 cattle in 2002 and about 4.8 million chickens in the same year. As a result, Turkmenistan exports various types of meat (beef, veal, mutton and poultry meat). The production of various types of meat in 2002 was 135,000 tonnes and in the same year, the production of milk was 0.83 million tonnes.

Mineral and Power Resources

Turkmenistan has one of the world's largest reserves of natural gas and petroleum. In 2002, it produced 53 billion cubic metres of natural gas, and 8.2 million metric tonnes of crude petroleum respectively. Turkmenistan is the fourth largest producer of gas in the world. Its reserves of gas and petroleum are estimated to be between 10 and 15 trillion cubic metre and 6.3 billion metric tonnes respectively. Oil wells are located on the Cheleken Peninsula and in the area of Nebit Dag. A large part of the increase in crude petroleum comes from Nebit Dag area by deeper drilling (Figure 13). There has been a controversy about the legal status of the Caspian Sea, and about the ownership of the extensive deposits of petroleum and natural gas beneath it. This controversy arose between Turkmenistan and other states connected with the Caspian Sea, e.g., Russia, Azerbaijan, Kazakhstan and Iran, in mid-1990. Although the sea was divided already into National Economic Zones, during the Soviet period, after 1992 there was demand for new demarcation. A conference was held in November 1996 at Ashgabat and a working group was constituted to formulate a new convention relating to the Caspian.

In 1993 Turkmenistan had an installed electrical capacity of 12 billion kilowatts, all of which was thermally produced by the country's two major thermal power stations (which was produced by the energy domestic natural gas). In 2002, 10.7 billion kilowatts of electricity was produced of which 20 per cent was exported while a proportion of the remaining electricity was distributed free of charge to domestic users. It was in 1996 that nominal charges were introduced but in 2003 budget, free distribution was provided.

In 1967, the first of the three 100 cm pipeline was completed from Central Asia to Moscow where it was connected with pipelines going to Leningrad and the Baltic Republics. This line collects gas from a chalk field in northern Turkmenistan on the west side of the Amu Darya. The other two lines also collect gas from the Darvaza and Bayram Ali fields. Together the three pipes carry about 30 billion cubic metre of gas per year to European Russia.

Industry

Textile (cotton, silk and woollen) are the leading industries of Turkmenistan. The production of woven fabrics in 1998 was 15 million sq metres, that of woven silk fabrics in the same year was 4,529 million sq metres and woollen fabrics in the same year was 2.5 million sq metres.

The production of blankets was 24,000 metric tonnes in 1998. The production of knotted wool carpets and rugs in 1998 was 315,000 sq metres. The production of footwear was 561,000 pairs in 1998. The production of nitrogen and phosphate fertilizers was 68,000 tonnes. The production of cement fertilizers was 487,000 metric tonnes in 2002 and the production of electrical energy was 10,700 million kilowatts in 2002.

The thermal power stations constitute the base for the electric power industry. These stations are well connected with towns in Ashgabat region. The river Murgab generates hydro-electricity and there are important stations on the river. Turkmenistan has a well-developed chemical industry. The industry produces sulphur from the sulphur mines of central Karakum and Gaurdak. In the Cheleken Peninsula, there is a 10 dine, bromine plant to extract bromine from the Kara-Bagaz-Gol on the Caspian Sea. There are super-phosphate plants at Chardzhou to extract phosphates.

Building material industry has made considerable headway. There are glass and brick factories in Ashgabat. There is a building material plant in Turkmenbashi (Krasnovodsk). There are metal working plants for the production of oil engines, agricultural equipments and consumer goods.

There is a tanning and footwear industry; the tannery is located at Mary and the footwear factory at Ashgabat.

Food Processing Industry

Turkmenistan has a developed food industry. In Dzhebel and Kuuli-Mayak, there are factories for the extraction and processing of table salt. Fishing industry is developed on the

Caspian Coast where motor-fishing stations are situated along with refrigeration plants. The production of all types of live catch is 12,792 metric tonnes.

Transport and Means of Communication

As a large part of Turkmenistan is arid, the means of communication and transport are confined to the south and south-western part. A railway from Uzbekistan in the east crosses Amu Darya at Farab near Chardzhou and moves towards south of Turkmenistan with an important station where a road from Mashad in Iran meets the railway and the road goes further north in Kara Kum desert for a distance of 160 km up to Darvaza. From Ashgabat the railway moves in a western direction to Turkmenbashi (Krasnovodsk) on the eastern coast of Caspian. In its journey from Ashgabat to Turkmenbashi it passes through Kizyl-Arvat where a road from Gorgan in Iran, joins it. Another road from Kizyl-Atrek joins the station Kazandzhik. Before reaching Turkmenbashi, it passes through another town-railway station in Nebit Dag (Figure 13).

Iran, owing to its geographical proximity has played an important role in the foreign relations of Turkmenistan to construct a railway between Iran and Turkmenistan. The railway which linked Turkmenistan city of Tejan with the northern Iranian city of Mashad was opened in 1996, thus affording access to Turkmenistan on the Gulf and to Istanbul (Turkey). Turkmenistan and Iran also signed an agreement for constructing a 200 km long gas pipeline between Korpeje in southern Turkmenistan and the city of Kord Kuy in Iran. The pipeline is planned to transport gas via Iran to Turkey and from there to Western Europe. The pipeline has been completed.

Turkmenbashi (Krasnovodsk), located on Caspian seashore is the site of a number of fishing centres and the railway is known as Trans-Caspian Railroad and from Mary railway station a branch goes to Kushka on the Afghan border.

Towns

Ashgabat is the capital of Turkmenistan. It is the cultural centre of Turkmenistan and seat of higher education. The railway from Ashgabat runs towards northwest and joins the port Turkmenbashi on the eastern coast of Caspian Sea. The train passes the following towns: (1) Geok-Tepe, (2) Bakharden (3) Kizyl-Arvat, (4) Kazandzhik, (5) Nebit Dag, and (6) Turkmenbashi (Figure 13).

Another branch goes towards east and joins Farab on the river Amu and passes through the following towns: (1) Mary, (2) Baryram Ali, and (3) Chardzhou located on Amu river (Figure 13).

Ashgabat is situated at the foot of the Kopet Dag mountain. It has beautiful straight streets and grand avenues in a plain area. There are magnificent houses surrounded by lush green orchards. The low hills are covered by pistachio and almond trees which separate Turkmenistan from Afghanistan and Iran. It has several cotton ginning and milling plants as well as silk spinning plants. It has several scientific research and higher educational institutions. Firyuza, near the Iranian border is the summer resort of Ashgabat. Situated at a distance of about 250 km west of Ashgabat Kizyl-Arvat, is an important engineering centre with locomotive and car repair shops.

Ashgabat was founded by the Russians in 1881, and till 1917, its name was spelled Askhabad; from 1920 to 1927, it was called Poltaratsk. Subsequently, its name became Ashkhabad and after independence its name changed to Ashgabat.

Roads branch off in different directions from Ashgabat as well as from Kizyl Arvat. There is one road which runs from Ashgabat to Mashad in Iran in the south, and another to Yerbent in the north in Turkmenistan and to Sernyy Zavod and a branch road goes to Darvaza in the Kara Kum desert.

Another road system runs from Kizyl Arvat to the southern border of Turkmenistan and joins the town of Kizyl Aterk and further south in the Iranian territory to Gorgan. (Figure 13).

Turkmenbashi (Krasnovodsk) is a major Caspian port located in a desert area. It is the terminus of the Trans-Caspian Railroad and a pipeline from the Nebit Dag petroleum fields goes to Turkmenbashi. It is a transhipment point for petroleum, cotton and salt. Nebit Dag on the Trans-Caspian Railway is linked with a rail spur to Vyshka, the oil field (Figure 13).

Further east of Ashgabat, lie the towns of Mary and Bayram Ali. Mary is a wool and cotton textile centre in the middle of Murab Oasis and lies on the Trans-Caspian Railroad. Other important industries which are located here are based on metal, food processing and carpet making. From Mary a branch railway parallel to Murghab for some distance runs south to Afghan border at Kushka.

Bayram Ali is located in the Mary Oasis on the Trans-Caspian railroad. It is a cotton centre with ginning mills, oil mills and soap factories.

Chardzhou is an important town at the junction of the railway, from Ashgabat and Tashauz in the north. It is a cotton and silk centre, and has metal works, fruit canning plants. Chardzhou enjoys a strategic location at the intersection of Amu Darya and the railroad. It has therefore become a very important river-rail transportation centre (Figure 13).

Kerki, in the east, is another important town and is known for cotton and livestock raising area. It has a variety of industries, cotton industry, meat packing and a leather industry.

Tashauz in the extreme north-east on the Uzbek border is situated in the Khorezm or Khiva Oasis, the eastern section of which falls in Uzbek state. Tashauz lies in the midst of an irrigated area which grows American short staple cotton and is an important centre for cattle and horse raising. Pristan Lavak on the Amu Darya serves as a port.

Trading Pattern

Exports (2002): Two items in Turkmenistan cover more than 96 per cent of its exports: (1) mineral fuel and lubricants, and (2) basic manufactures (Table 8).

Table 8

Turkmenistan: Principal Commodities

(in US million dollar)

Exports	*2000*	*2001*	*2002*
Crude material (inedible) except fuel	257.1	123.7	83.8 (3.1%)
Mineral fuels, lubricants, etc.	2029.7	2217.2	2447.1 (91%)
Basic manufactures	107.0	141.6	150.6 (5.5%)
Machinery and transport equipment	15.5	14.5	17.1 (.63%)
Total (including others)	2409.3	2497.0	2698.6

Imports (2002): In the matter of imports, about half the total value of imports consisted of machinery and transport equipments. A little more then one-fifth of the total value of imports was of basic manufactures; of the remaining three-tenths 30 per cent of the total consisted of food and live animals, beverage and tobacco, chemicals, marine fuels and lubricants and miscellaneous manufactured articles (Table 9).

Table 9

Turkmenistan: Principal Commodities

(in US million dollar)

Import	*2000*	*2001*	*2002*
Food and live animals	180.4	129.4	114.3 (6.4%)
Beverages and tobacco	25.2	56.8	70.1 (4.0%)
Minerals fuel, lubricant	21.3	39.1	25.7 (1.4%)
Chemicals	159.0	178.6	210.8 (11.9%)
Basic manufactures	382.4	448.7	394.2 (22.0%)
Machinery and transport equipment	782.5	1204.7	857.6 (48.0%)
Miscellaneous manufactured articles	111.1	128.1	112.7 (6.3 %)
Total (including others)	1651.9	2185.4	1785.4

Trading Partners

Exports (2002): Half of the total value of exports went to two countries: Iran and Ukraine and one-sixth to Azerbaijan. Thus, two-thirds of the value of export of Turkmenistan went to three countries: Iran, Ukraine and Azerbaijan. The one-third of the value of exports went to seven countries, namely, Afghanistan, Germany, Kazakhstan, Russia, Switzerland, Tajikistan and Turkey (Table 10).

Table 10

Turkmenistan: Principal Trading Partners

(in US million dollar)

Exports	*2000*	*2001*	*2002*
Afghanistan	38.0	42.0	45.5 (5.5%)
Azerbaijan	37.1	122.9	133.4 (16.2%)
Germany	404.8	5.8	10.5 (1.2%)
Iran	242.0	241.0	199.9 (24.3%)
Kazakhstan	5.3	70.5	76.5 (9.3%)
Russia	1029.3	35.5	23.4 (2.9%)
Switzerland	91.9	0.8	0.8 (.9%)
Tajikistan	29.1	56.6	61.5 (7.5%)
Turkey	186.0	65.2	70.8 (8.7%)
Ukraine	164.9	182.1	197.6 (24.1%)
Total (including others)	2228.4	822.4	819.9

Imports (2002): About 70 per cent of imports of Turkmenistan came from four countries: Germany, Ukraine, Russia and UAE. The remaining 30 per cent of imports came from six countries, namely, France, Iran, Japan, Turkey, USA and Uzbekistan (Table 11).

Table 11
Turkmenistan: Principal Trading Partners

(in US million dollar)

Import	*2000*	*2001*	*2002*
France	75.7	50.5	67.6 (5.4%)
Germany	52.6	140.6	273.9 (22%)
Iran	90.9	98.1	104.3 (8.3%)
Japan	144.4	35.9	6.0 (0.5%)
Russia	254.5	153.4	152.3 (12.2%)
Turkey	253.3	115.8	125.7 (10.0%)
Ukraine	214.3	235.7	255.8 (20.5%)
UAE	146.6	158.2	168.2 (13.5%)
USA	62.8	273.4	51.9 (4.1%)
Uzbekistan	35.3	38.8	42.1 (3.4%)
Total (including others)	1330.4	1300.4	1247.8

4

Uzbekistan

Among the Central Asian states, Uzbekistan has been famous for producing outstanding persons in diverse fields: poetry, astronomy, architecture, and medicine. Its contribution to world civilization is immense and cities such as Tashkent, Samarkand and Bukhara are well known for art and culture. High quality of silk and cotton, the famous Karakul wool and metal sculpture, they all come from these parts. It is the most populous and well developed among the states of Central Asia. Its area is 447,400 sq km and its total population was 26,479,000 (2004), about 45.39 per cent of the total population of all the five states of Central Asia. It contains half the sown area of all the states, 80 per cent of the cotton area of all the states and two-thirds of railroad area.

On its west lies Turkmenistan and the Amu Darya in the west forms the natural boundary. In the north lie Kazakhstan and the Aral Sea, in the east its boundary is highly zigzag and includes parts of the Kyzl-Kum desert, the Tien Shan ranges and the Fargana valley, while in the south lies Afghanistan. Probably no other country in the world has boundaries so irregular as Uzbekistan (Figure 14). The Uzbeks live in ancient

Figure 14
Uzbekistan

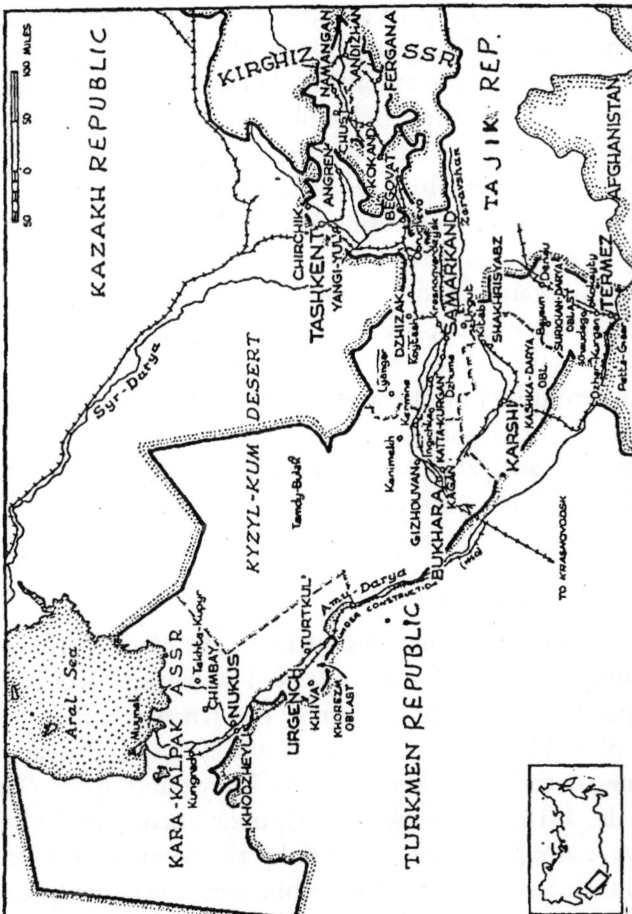

Source: Shabad Theodore, 1961, *Geography of the USSR*, New York, p. 389.

oases that formed around rivers coming down from various mountain ranges and flowing in different directions. Scattered over a huge area, these oases – the Tashkent, the Fargana, the Zarafshan, and the Karshka Darya, the Surkhan Darya and the Khorezm – are separated by arid steppes deserts and mountain ranges. The reason for its complicated boundary in the eastern section is that in the east, Soviet Union gave the people of Central Asia the opportunity to delineate boundaries in accordance with living ethnic principles, dividing the Uzbeks, Tajik, Turkmen, Kirghis, and Kazakhs in accordance with the territory they actually inhabited. In addition to the ethnic consideration, in delineating the boundaries, the sources of water supply had also been taken into consideration. The mountain water-divide, which had provided water to the Uzbeks for centuries, was also taken into account. The consideration of national interest is one of the reasons why there is no national conflict in Central Asia (Figure 14). In 2002, the Majlis adopted a resolution and elected Islam A. Karimov for a five-year term. Uzbekistan is a secular democratic presidential republic. In late March 2004, there was an outbreak of widespread violence, the motives for which were unclear.

Historical Background

The Uzbeks claim their decent from the Mongol tribes, who migrated to Central Asia, adopted sedentary occupation in Central Asia in the 13th century. The Khanate tribes occupied most of Bukhara and Samarkand, the Kokand. Russian forces conquered the lands between Syr Darya and Amu Darya in 1886. In 1918, the Turkestan republic including Uzbekistan was proclaimed as part of USSR by the Soviet forces. In 1924, the Uzbek Soviet Socialist Republic was proclaimed, including (until 1992), the Tajik Republic. In 1990, the Supreme Soviet adopted a declaration of sovereignty and in 1991 Uzbekistan declared its sovereignty and proclaimed an independent Republic. Earlier in 1990, Islam Karimov was elected executive President and subsequently as President of the cabinet of ministers. In 1992, Uzbekistan was declared a secular state. Commonwealth of Independent States (CIS) was established in 1991 and Uzbekistan became a full member of CIS, but it maintained close links with the other four Central Asian states.

Uzbekistan took a laudable step to protect the environment and save the Aral Sea from the ecological hazard by participating in a meeting of all the five Republics in January 1994, and agreeing to a joint fund and the establishment of a permanent committee to examine and attempt to redress the ecological damage to the Aral Sea and also to improve the health of those living in the region. In February 1997, at a summit meeting in Kazakhstan, each republic pledged 0.3 per cent of its respective budgets for the common fund.

The prosperity of Uzbekistan depends on the numerous oases in the state. The most important oasis is the Fargana Valley which is the largest and exceptionally fertile land, measuring approximately 300 km in length and 100 km in width with greater portion lying in Uzbekistan (Figure 15). Other important oases are Tashkent, Samarkant, Bukhara and Khiva. The Fergana oasis is irrigated by Syr Darya and many other streams coming from the Thien Shan mountain. The Samarakand and Bukhara oases are drained by the Zeravshan river which is supposed to be the tributary of Amu Darya, but it is lost in sand before reaching that river. The Khiva or Khorezm oasis is bounded by the Turkmenistan Republic in the south and the Kara Kalpak Autonomous Republic in the north.

Uzbekistan has a varied topography. In the east lies the western spurs of Tien Shan which encloses the exceptionally fertile plain of Fergana Valley. The extensive Kyzyl Kum (Red Sand), which includes the Kara Kalpak Autonomous Republic, extends north-westward and much of the area is desert. The desert of Kyzyl Kum extends for about 450 km and the sand has been stabilized largely by the sparse vegetation. There are few

Figure 15
Fergana Valley

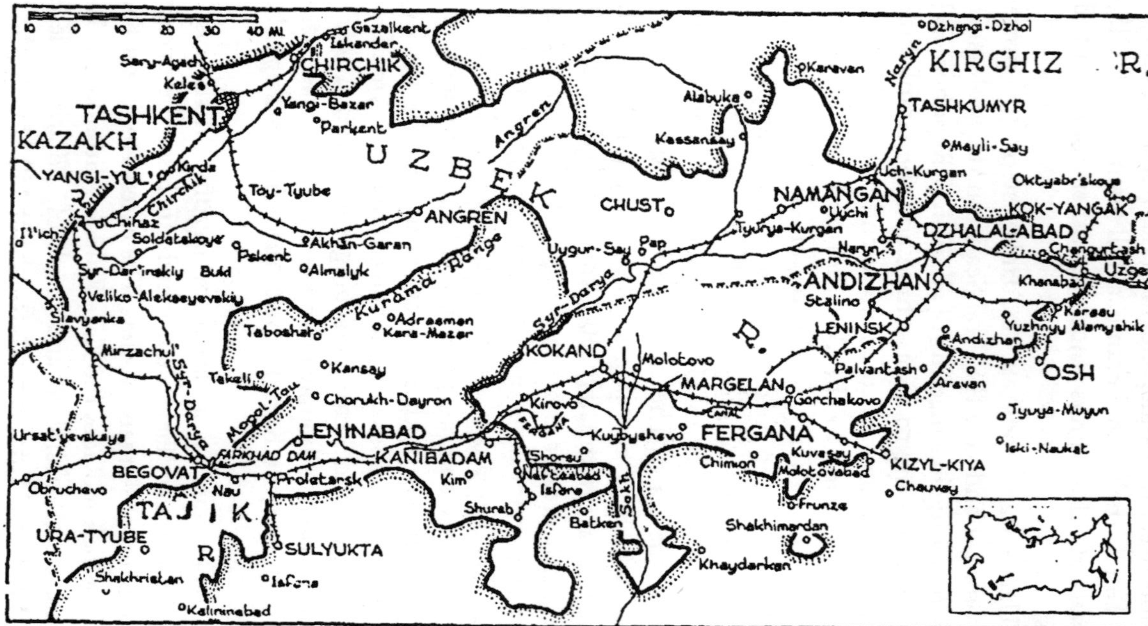

Source: Ibid, p. 395.

sand dunes in this desert. The Kara Kalpak Republic includes the southern and western portion of Aral Sea.

Rising from the Pamirs, the Amu Darya skirting the northern boundary of Afghanistan in the south of Uzbekistan with numerous braded channels joins the Aral Sea in Kara Kalpak. During the summer when the snow melts on the mountains, the volume of the river swells while in the winters it shrinks. The river spreads much debris and makes a wide flood plain over which it flows. The delta of the river begins from Nukus, to a distance of about 150 km.

The topography in the east is highly complex. One encounters a number of alluvial fans fringing the foothills. To the northeast of Tashkent lie the Chitkal ranges which feed the Chirchik and Angren rivers. These rivers provide water to the oasis of Tashkent before joining Syr Darya (Figure 14).

Climate

The climate of Uzbekistan is continental with hot and dry summers and cold winters. The average January temperature is below freezing (–2°C) and the average July temperature varies between 25 and 35°C. The average yearly rainfall varies between 5 and 7 cm in the lowland and 25 and 30 cm in the foothill areas. In the summers over the mountains, the rainfall may be as much as 60 cm. Local winds are important. The valleys and foothills may be warmed in the winter by the foehn winds descending from the Tien Shan. In the south, near the Afghan border, Termez receives cold dusty wind – 'Afganets' the cold wind blow for over two months from the high mountains in the winter and spring.

Vegetation

The scanty rainfall has led to sparse vegetation and in the Kyzyl Kum desert there is practically no natural vegetation. In the spring months, with a little rain, some vegetation sprouts here and there, but it vanishes with the advent of the hot scorching summer. In the sandy areas shrubs like *juzgun* (alligo num) and the white *saxaul* grow, while in saline clayey areas, *black saxaul,* (bayalych) shrubs can stand to the dry conditions. Along the banks of rivers one comes across poplars, small willows and olive trees. High up in the mountains at an altitude of 1,500 metres, one comes across permanent meadows and junipers and deciduous trees of walnut, maple and apricot and above 1,500 metres there are conifers.

Irrigation

The Uzbeks have known the art of irrigation from times immemorial. Irrigation by canal has been carried out in the oases. The Fergana Valley is irrigated by the Syr Darya and many other smaller streams that come down from the mountains. Further west, the Tashkent oasis is drained by the Chirchik and Angren rivers and the tributaries of the Syr Darya. The Samarkand and Bukhara oases are drained by the Zeravshan river which is not able to reach the Amu River and disappears in the desert.

Mention should be made of Great Fergana canal which was completed in 1939. The main canal system is 320 km long and completely encircles the Fergana Basin. Many feeder canals distribute the water over much of the Basin floor. The canal irrigates more than 0.8 million hectares. Another irrigation canal Namangan, on the northern side of the Basin, parallel to the Great Fergana canal, has been constructed which irrigates an additional area of over 30,000 hectares.

It may be noted that Farkhad Dam was constructed in the 1940s opposite to the city of Bakabad (Begovat) in the western part of the Fergana Basin where Syr Darya passes through a gorge on its way to the Hungry Steppe to the west. The Farkhad Dam provides hydroelectricity to the synthetic and chemical industries located in the Fergana Valley. The dam also provides irrigation to the 'cotton island' in the Hungry Steppe.

It would be interesting to mention a legend behind the naming of Farkhad Dam. According to Uzbek lore, a capricious princess once lived on the high cliff that overlooked the dam site. She agreed to give her hand in marriage to one who performed the greatest deed. She announced that she would marry the man who could bring water to the Hungry Steppe. One cunning young nobleman ordered the steppe to be covered with mats of chi grass. When the sun rose in the morning, its glare from the Chi grass looked very much like the reflection from a water surface. The princess agreed to marry the hero on the spot. Meanwhile a simple hero of common people had brought water from the mountains to the steppes by his honest toil. But it was too late. The princess had already married the cheat. Farkhad (in some versions, was called Farhad), as the honest peasant was called. When he learnt the trickery, he threw his heavy Ketmen, a hoc like spade, into the air, which fell on his head and broke his skull. Farkhad had brought water to the desert, but the Uzbek peasant could not marry the princess (Shireen).[1]

Agriculture

Agriculture in Uzbekistan is subtropical in character and the determining factors are temperature and rainfall. The frost-free period is generally 180 to 230 days, the summer is rainless and almost all the days in July and August are sunny days. Cotton is the most important crop. Fergana Valley, the Hungry Steppe and Zeravshan Valley are the main regions of cotton production owing to the availability of irrigation water in the summer months. The farmers follow a rotation of crops and cotton is followed by lucerne, maize, rice and jute. The yield per hectare is high owing to heavy application of chemical fertilizers and manures. The silt deposited by irrigation water is effective in augmenting the yield, and the production of cotton lint in 2002 was 1.008 million tonnes. Of the total area of about 45 million hectares, about 4 million hectares are arable, 20 million hectares are permanent pastures and about 1.5 million hectares are forest lands. Table 12 shows the production of principal crops in thousand metric tonnes in Uzbekistan.

It will be seen from table that there has been a sharp increase over the years in the production of wheat. In the

Table 12
Principal Crops

(in 000 metric tonnes)

Crops	*2000*	*2001*	*2002*
Wheat	3521.7	3786	4956
Rice	154.8	67.8	143.1
Barley	79	57	171.5
Maize	131.4	100	225.4
Sorghum	20	15	18.8
Potatoes	730.1	735.5	730
Sugarbeet	215	104	-
Beans	14	12	15
Sunflower seed	12	10.3	10.5
Sesame seed	20	15.5	15
Cotton seed	1803	1830	1850
Other Oil seed	8.5	8.6	8
Cabbages	877.5	921.4	900
Tomatoes	994.2	1040	1000
Cucumber	270.5	284.2	280
Onion	146.2	153.6	150
Garlic	24.8	26.1	25
Carrot	33.8	40	40
Other vegetables	287	301	311
Apple	497.3	500.2	500
Pear	22.3	22.6	23
Apricot	43	43	43
Cherries	19.8	21.2	20
Peaches	47	47.5	45
Plums	99.5	101	100
Grapes	624.2	573.8	570
Watermelon	451.4	459.9	460
Other fruits and berries	42.1	42.9	-
Tobacco	19	19	18
Jute	20	21	20
Cotton lint	1000	1015	1008

Source: Europa, Vol. II (2004), p. 4619.

foothills the abundant rain water is used in wheat cultivation in the early spring, and by the onset of the dry season the sowing of the wheat crop is completed. However, the increase in the production of other crops is not significant.

The production of maize declined but this soon picked up, while there is some increase in the production of potatoes. The republic is noted for its fruits. Grapes, apricots, apples, peaches, pears, sweet cherries almonds, figs and pomegranate are some of the fruits cultivated in Uzbekistan. Cotton is the most important crop and in spite of fluctuations in the area over the years the production is substantial. As much as 60 per cent of Uzbekistan's land is covered by desert and steppes but the massive irrigation of desert areas has greatly increased the production of cotton and Uzbekistan is the fifth largest producer of cotton in the world and the crop accounts for more than 40 per cent of the value of total agricultural production. In 2002, agriculture including forestry contributed 34.6 per cent of GDP and the agriculture sector employed one-third of the total working population. Cotton accounted for about half of the value of the total exports. The government has tried to reduce the area under cultivation of cotton in order to produce more grain. Table 12 shows the production of principal crops.

Mineral Resources

Uzbekistan is well endowed with mineral resources. Some of the best deposits of coal occur in the Fergana Valley and in the hilly country around it. The deposits at Angren, where lignite is mined, is important in the industrial development of Uzbekistan. The country produced 2.73 million tonnes of coal in 2002. There are large reserves of gold, silver, uranium, copper, lead, zinc and tungsten. Uzbekistan is the fourth largest producer of uranium in the world. In 2000, 2,054 metric tonnes of Uranium were produced. The Navoi uranium mine was expected to increase production by about 40 per cent in response to overseas demand. All uranium mined is exported. Uzbekistan is the sixth largest producer of gold in the world and the Murantau mine in the Kyzyl Kum desert is the world's largest single open cast gold mine, producing some 70 per cent of Uzbekistan's average annual output of 62,276 kilogram of gold in 2000. In 1995, it was announced that the Amantaytau and Daugistau with estimated reserves of million metric tonnes of gold were being developed. Altynak on the slopes of the Kurama mountain in the Fergana Valley and the Kochbulak mine in the same area and Zarafshan complex in the central part of Kyzyl Kum desert are all producers of gold. Annual output of gold is about 85 metric tonnes.

Sulphur is mined at shorsu in the Fergana Valley and forms the basis of chemical industry. Zinc and copper refineries are established at the Almalyk mine. Tungsten and molybdenum are mined at Lyangar in Samarkand provinces. Table 13 shows the production of various minerals.

Table 13
Minerals

(in metric tonnes)

	1998	*1999*	*2000*	*2001*
Copper ore	-	91000	91000	
Tungsten ore	200	-	-	
Molybdenum ore	350	350	350	
Silver ore (kg)	70000	86000	89000	
Uranium ore	2000	2159	2054	
Gold (kg)	80000	66028	62276	85.4(metric tonnes)

Source: Europa, Volume II, 2004, p. 4620.

Power Resources

Petroleum is obtained in the Fergana Valley. Oil and natural gas fields are found near Andizhan. Other oilfields are at Chimion, and Shorsu, in the southern part of the valley. In the Surkhan Darya province, petroleum is produced in the south-east of the republic. In 2002 Uzbekistan produced 7.2 million tonnes of crude oil, and natural gas 58,000 million cubic metres, the same year.

There are enormous reserve of gas in Uzbekistan. The Gazlifeild in 1965-66 produced 22 billion m^3 of gas and supplied to Ural industries, 2,000 km away by means of pipelines. A new city Navoi was established in the vicinity of Gazli field which uses the gas for the production of thermal electricity, nitrogenous fertilizers and synthetic fibres.[2]

Large hydroelectric schemes were established as early as in 1960s and 1970s on Syr Darya for irrigation as well as for hydroelectricity on the Farkhad and the Charadra dam. In 2000, 72 per cent of electricity was generated by natural gas, 12 per cent was produced by hydroelectricity and 11 per cent by petroleum (Table 14 shows the power resources of Uzbekistan).

Table 14
Power Resources

	2001	*2002*
Coal	2711000	2731000 metric tonnes
Petroleum	7256000	7241000 metric tonnes
Gas	57000	58000 million cu metres

Source: Europa, Vol. II, 2004, p. 4620.

Industry

As Uzbekistan is the most important producer of cotton among the Central Asian states, and most of it comes from Fergana Valley, cotton mills have been established at Tashkent, and at Fergana. Tashkent is not only the capital of Uzbekistan but its extensive irrigation facilities helps the production in large quantities of cotton and it has become an important industrial centre for cotton textile industry. During the Second World War a second industrial hub was created at Begovat. Other light industries are silk manufacturing, paper industry and chemical industry. In 2000 it produced 360 million sq metre of fabrics, 13,100 tonnes of paper, 1.3 million tonnes of mineral fertilizer. The cotton and silk mills are located at Margelan and

Kokand, while the cement works are at Kuvasay in the Fergana province (oblast). The chemical works are at Shorsu.

A big mill is located at Begovat, a copper refinery at Almalyk. Tashkent has agricultural implement works and shoe plants; 26,000 TV sets, 1,000 refrigerators were produced in 2000 and 10,300 washing machines in 1998. There is a famous electro-chemical centre at Chirchic on the Chirchic river north-east of Tashkent. It produces nitrogenous fertilizer and related chemicals for the chemical industry. It is also the site of large hydroelectric station.

Bukhara is famous for Karakul wool processing. Nakus in the Karakalpak Republic in Uzbekistan is known for meat packing and flour milling. Table 15 shows industrial development of Uzbekistan from 2000 to 2002.

Table 15

Industries

	2000	*2001*	*2002*
Cigarettes (million)	1766	-	-
Woven Cotton Fabric (million sq m)	360	-	-
Electrical Energy	56401	47961 (KWh million)	-
Cement (tonnes)	3331000	3722000	3927000 tonnes

Source: Europa, Vol. II, 2004, p. 4620.

Towns

The important towns of Uzbekistan are: Tashkent, Samarkand, Bukhara, Khiva, Nukus, and Fergana. Other smaller towns are Andizham, Namangan, Angreen, Begovat, Dzhizak, Termez, Karshi, Chirchik.

Tashkent: Tashkent is the capital of Uzbekistan. Its total population in 2004 was 3,394,000 and it is situated on the north-western edge of Fergana Valley, close to the foothills. It is the largest and one of the oldest cities of Central Asia at the junction of many historic routes. It is a large industrial centre with iron and steel industry, manufacturing agricultural machinery, cotton textile, silk industry, clothing factories and shoe plants. It has a flourishing food industry including meat packing, flour milling, and fruit and vegetable canning. It is a very old city founded in the 7th century AD and became the capital of Uzbekistan in 1930.

Tashkent lies in the centre of an extensive oasis which is watered by the Chirchick, the right-hand tributary of Syr Darya. The *ariq*, the secondary canal carries water all over the city. The ariqs run on both sides of every street and the branch ariqs carry the water into the compound of the houses and provide water for all the vegetation in which Tashkent is so rich.

Structurally, the city can be divided into two parts: old and new Tashkent. The old town is a chaos of narrow winding street between the windowless earthen walls of the Uzbeck houses. At the street crossings there are small tea houses where one sits on a carpet and gets a refreshing drink of green tea.

The new town was built by the Russians when Tashkent was a part of Russian empire some 130 years ago. The streets are wide and straight. The houses are small, facing the street. However, today both the old as well as the new town have considerably changed. Many big buildings have come up in the new town and the main streets have been asphalted. In the old town, big buildings of modern architecture have been built.

Tashkent is a city of flowers and fruits. In the market place one comes across heaps of fruits and vegetables and large quantities of flowers. All summer there is an abundance of fruits. In May, there are strawberries, in June apricots, in July peaches, in August grapes and melons.

There is a big flourishing textile industry. The warm dry climate is highly favourable for the industry.

Tashkent is the most important cultural centre of Central Asia. A large number of Central Asian higher education institutions are found in Tashkent.[3]

Samarkand (population: 550,000) (2004): It is the capital of Samarkand province. It is drained by Zeravshan river and in the north of the province lie Nura Tau range and Ak Tau range. Samarkhand is a cotton ginning and silk spinning centre. It has also clothing and shoe factories. It is the oldest city of Central Asia and dates from 3rd or 4th century BC. It was the capital of Uzbek from 1925-1930 (Figure 14).

Bukhara (population: 389,960) (2004): It is the capital of Bukhara province. This is the biggest province of Uzbekistan and includes a large section of the Kyzyl Kum Desert. It has Karakul wool processing industry, silk spinning and clothing manufacturing factories. Bukhara is an old centre of Islamic culture (Figure 14).

Namangan (population: 420,000) (2004): It is the capital of the province Namangan which occupies the entire northern part of the Fargana Valley, and is located on the headstream 'Narya river'. It has a well developed cotton and silk industry.

Andizhan (population: 400,950) (2004) 1990: It is the capital of the province Andhizhan which is the eastern part of the Fergana Valley and is drained by the Kara Darya, a tributary of Syr Darya. It is an important railway centre and connects Namangan and other towns of Kirghiz republic. It has cotton ginning and cotton seed-oil extracting industries, food processing plants and metal works.

Fergana (population: 268,000) (2004): It is the capital of the province of Fergana and covers the north-western portion of Fergana Valley. A large portion of its southern section is irrigated by numerous streams coming from the Alay range with a network of canals.

Fergana is an important centre of cotton and silk textile industry, cotton seed oil mill, clothing factories and large power plants. The town was founded in 1876.

Kokand (population: 246,000) (2004): It is an ancient city and was once a modern industrial centre. It has superphosphate plant and cotton and silk processing industry. It produces refined beetsugar.

Nukus (population: 237,600) (2004): It is the capital of the province of Kara Kalpak. In 1925 it was the capital of autonomous province and part of Kazakhstan. In 1936, it became part of Uzbekistan. Kara Kalpak is a desert area and the Amu delta divides it into two parts, eastern and western. It includes a portion of Kyzyl-Kum desert, and only the Amu Darya Valley and delta have irrigated agriculture. Formerly Turtkul was the capital but when it was threatened by Amu Darya floods, Nukus became the capital. It has cotton textile and leather factories (Figure 14).

Karshi (population: 221,000) (2004): Karshi is known for its food processing industry, also for its metal works. It lies in the south-west of Uzbekistan at some distance south of Bukhara.

Chirrchik (population: 214,000) (2004): It lies close to Tashkent. It is an important centre of railway and provides a route to Kyrgyzstan. It is a major electro-chemical centre of Uzbekistan on the Chirchik river (north-west of Tashkent). It produces nitrogenous fertilizers and machinery for chemical industry. It is the site of a large hydroelectric station.

Angren (population: 199,550) (2004): It is situated in the east of Tashkent and constitutes the largest coal mining centre of Central Asia. It was developed during the Second World War and makes substantial contribution to the four million tonnes of coal produced in Uzbekistan. It is linked by rail and a coal gas pipeline with Tashkent and furnishes coaking coal to the Begovat steel mill.

Just upstream from the Farkhad Dam on the Syr Darya lies the Kayrak-Kum, 'hydro knot' with its *Druzhba Narodov*, i.e., friendship of Nation hydroelectric station which was completed in 1957, based on the reservoir which is 70 km long within the neck of Tajikistan that extends into the western end of the Fergana Basin. This reservoir feeds 12 canals which irrigate half a million arid land, 0.3 million of which lie in the Hungry Steppe, west of the Fergana Basin in Uzbek Republic.

A canal about 240 km in length along the left bank of the Syr Darya has added 0.2 million hectare of new rice land.

The Pakhta Aral (cotton island) near Farkhid Dam is a huge cotton growing area and extends into Kazakhstan and derives its irrigation water from the extensive irrigation network of canals and various reservoirs. As a result, the territory was transferred from the Kazakh Republic to Uzbek Republic in 1963. This action was taken in order to place the area under the jurisdiction of one political unit to facilitate development and management of the irrigation district.

Urgench (population: 175,000) (2004): Urgench is the capital of Khorezm province which falls in the Khorezm oasis, also known as Khiva oasis. It lies to the north of Turkmenistan and south of Kalpak Republic. The province is well irrigated and produces large quantity of cotton and silk.

The chief city is Khiva, a historic city and was the capital of Khorazm for a long time and a centre of cotton industry; it has also a carpet and metal working industry.

Margelan (population: 169,000) (2004): It lies in the Fergana Valley and very close to the railway that connects Uzbekistan with Tajikistan, Turkmenistan and Kyrgystan and is famous for cotton and silk factories.

Almalyk (population: 157,000) (2004): It is famous for a copper and zinc refinery.

Patterns of Trade

Exports: The major exports of Uzbekistan in 2000 was cotton fibre which covered 49.2 per cent of total value of the exports. Energy products covered 18.3 per cent of the total value of exports consisted metal which covered 11.80 per cent. The remaining exports consisted of food products (9.6 per cent), machinery and equipment (6.06 per cent), and chemical and plastics (5.10 per cent) (Table 18).

Imports: As regards imports, of the total value nearly half of imports was covered by machinery and equipment. About one-fourth by meals and food products and the remaining one-fourth was covered by chemical and energy. The total imports in 2002 were of 2160.9 million US $; of this about half was covered by machinery and equipment. One-fourth by metals and food products and the remaining one-fourth by chemical, plastics and energy products (Table 17).

Table 16

Industry: Selected Products

(in 000 metric tonnes, unless otherwise stated)

	1998	*1999*	*2000*	*2001*	*2002*
Cigarette (million)	7582	10668	7766		
Wool yarn (pure and mixed)	02	03	03		
Cotton yarn (pure and mixed)	105	105	135		
Woven cotton fabrics (million sq metres)	314	333	360		
Sulphuric acid	856	897	823		
Nitrogen fertilizer	755	707	717		
Phosphate fertilizer	141	169	117		
Motor spirit (petrol)	1603	1638	1709		
Gas diesel distillate fuel oil	2227	2220	1900		
Residual fuel oils	1977	1750	1700		
Lubricating oils	229	223	238		
Cement (Thousand metric tonnes)	3331	3284	3722	3722	3927
Domestic refrigerators (000)	16	2	1		
Domestic washing machines (000)	05	-	-		
Television (000)	192	50	26		
Electric energy (KWh)	54790	55581	56401		47961

Source: Europa, Vol. II, 2004, p. 4620.

Table 17

Principal Commodities

(in U.S. million $)

Import	*1998*	*1999*	*2000*
Chemical and plastics	407.2	363	399.5 (19.3)
Metals	303.6	245.4	253.5 (12.7)
Machinery and equipment	1553.7	1393.5	1044.1 (49.7)
Food products	712.2	408.1	351.1 (12.7)
Energy products	16.30	66.6	112.7 (5.4)
Total	2993	2476.6	2160.9

Source: Europa, Vol. II, 2004, p. 4621.

Note: Figures in parentheses show percentage computed by the author.

Table 18
External Trade: Principal Commodities

(in US million dollars)

Export	*1998*	*1999*	*2000*
Cotton fibre	1361	883.7	897.1
Chemical and plastics	51.7	101.8	93.4
Metal	180.7	138.9	216.7
Machinery and equipment	146.6	103.2	111.8
Food products	111.9	206.7	176.4
Energy products	277.8	371.5	335.2
Total	2129.7	1805.8	1830.6

Trading Partners

Exports: Uzbekistan exported goods to three Central Asian countries: namely Kazakhstan, Kyrgyzstan and Tajikistan to the tune of 22.9 million US dollars, i.e., a little less the one-fourth of the total exports in 2002. Its exports went to three European countries to the tune 22.8, again a little less the one fourth of the total value of exports.

To Commonwealth Independent States (CIS), Russia and Ukraine had the lion's share of 40.9 per cent of the total value of exports. The remaining 13.4 per cent of value of exports went to Korea, and Turkey combined (Table 19).

Import: With regards to imports, one-fourth (25.9) of the value of imports went to Russia. The import from the three Central Asian countries was low, to the tune of 16.5 million US $. Uzbekistan imported from two European countries: France and Germany and the combined import was 13.5. From Ukraine the import was 8.0 and from USA 8.1, Korea 22 and Turkey 6.0 per cent (Table 20).

Table 19

Principal Trading Partners

(in US million dollars)

Export	*2000*	*2001*	*2002*	*2002 (%)*
Germany	67.6	56.4	44.2	3.4
Italy	172.8	155.2	157.7	12.4
Kazakhstan	66.6	72.9	79.1	6.2
Korea	94.5	124.3	134.9	10.6
Kyrgyzstan	68.4	60.7	63.6	5.0
Poland	36.7	82.3	89.3	7.0
Russia	602	527	327.8	25.8
Tajikistan	168.7	137	148.7	11.7
Turkey	78	32.8	35.6	2.8
Ukraine	161.8	178	193.2	15.1
Total	1517.1	14266	1274.1	100.0

Table 20

Principal Trading Partners

(in US million dollars)

Import	*2000*	*2001*	*2002*	*2002 (%)*
France	73.4	118.8	42.8	2.3
Germany	233.3	227.2	211.4	11.2
Kazakhstan	163.1	163.7	177.6	9.4
Kyrgyzstan	98.3	52.7	31.5	1.6
Korea	253.5	380.3	412.7	22.0
Russia	301.9	400.2	486.9	25.9
Tajikistan	107.6	95.9	104.1	5.5
Turkey	90.9	98.7	107.1	6.0
Ukraine	125.4	138.4	150.3	8.0
USA	182.7	162.5	151.9	8.1
Total	1630.1	1838.4	1876.3	100.0

Notes

1. Paul, E. Lydolph (1969), *Geography of USSR*, New York, p. 249.
2. Paul, E. Lydolph (1969), *Geography of USSR*, New York, p. 256.
3. Mikhailov, Nicholas (1948) *Soviet Russia – The Land and Its People*, New York, pp. 273-275.

5

Tajikistan

Historical Background

The evolution of the state of Tajikistan had a chequered history. The Tajik ethnic groups, which inhabited the regions of Bukhara and Turkestan, were constituted as a unit and admitted as a republic of the Soviet Union in 1929. The Tajik as an ethnic group differed from the Turkie tribes as they followed a sedentary lifestyle and spoke the Persian language. Before 1929, the Tajik Soviet Socialist Republic was established as a part of the Uzbek Soviet Socialist Republic. In 1991, after the failure of *coup d'etat* in Moscow, in September, the Tajik Supreme Soviet proclaimed Tajikistan an independent state and the name of the country was changed to the Republic of Tajikistan. In December 1991, the Republic became a member of the CIS.

There was a general demonstration and civil war against the communist government which was replaced by a revolutionary coalition council and owing to the civil war that ensued, a peace keeping force by CIS was stationed in Tajikistan and a state of emergency was imposed in early 1993.

On 23, December 1996 a cease fire was signed between President Rakhmonov and the insurgent leader Sayed Abdullah Nuri. There was another agreement in March, 1997 for the disarmament of the insurgents and they were integrated into the regular armed forces.

Tajikistan has a presidential system of government. Imamalis Sharopovich Rakhmonov was elected president on November 6, 1994 for a period of five years. He was re-elected for another term of seven years on 6 November, 1999. The majority of the people are adherents to Islam but the state's declared policy is secularism. In the north and west of Tajikistan lie Uzbekistan and Kyrgyzstan and in the east is China. In the south, it is bordered by Afghanistan.

Its total area[1] is 143,100 sq km with a population of 6,298,000 in 2004.[2]

Topography

Tajikistan is a mountainous country. Its south-eastern portion is formed by Pamir Alay range called as the "roof of the world", Stalin peak is over 8,000 metres and another high peak, though a little less high, is named Lenin peak which is a little over 7,000 metres and Karl Mary peak is slightly lower than Mt. Lenin. In the valley below, lies the Kara Kul lake at an elevation of 4,000 metres and south of Mt. Stalin lies the Fedchenko glacier, 80 km long, one of the largest glaciers in the world.

The western section of the mountains contains deep narrow ravines while the eastern Pamir is the highest section of the mountain with almost no ravines, but a number of bowl shaped valleys strewn with patches of grass. The valleys are at a height of 4,500 metres.

The northern part of Tajikistan is drained by the Syr Darya while the other rivers of the republic, the Zeravshan drain into the Amu Darya system. The Darya rises in the Afghan-Hindu Kush and forms most of the frontier between Afghan and Tajikistan.

The Vakhan Darya which almost forms the southern boundary of Tajikistan is joined by the tributary river Pamir. Vakhan Darya flows towards west and taking a sharp bend of U-shape flows towards north forming the boundary between Tajikistan and Afghanistan and is known as Panj and further west of Tajikistan, it is also known as Amu Darya and receives the tributary Kafirnigan which in its upper course in Kyrgyzstan is called Kyzyl-su and further west in Tajikistan as Surkhab river. Mention should be made of Murgab river which rises in the extreme east near the border of China and joins Panj river at Rushan. Another river Zeravshan which rises near the border of Kyrgyzstan in the north of Tajikistan flows towards west (Figure 16).

Several important canals have been taken out from these rivers which form the base of extensive irrigation system particularly in the Vakhsh and Zeravshan valleys.

Climate

The climate of Tajikistan is much influenced by its varied topography and its distance from the sea. The climate of the lowlands is dry continental with average temperature of 32°C in July and 3°C to 4°C in January and an yearly rainfall of 25 cm. In the foothills up to a height of about 200 metres the climate is cool and humid with average temperature of 16 to 18°C in summers and below freezing in winters, with an yearly rainfall of 50 cm. Above 3 to 4 thousand metres, the climate is very harsh with snow and glaciers occupying permanent position and average yearly temperature is below freezing.

Irrigation

Irrigation has transformed agriculture in Tajikistan. Major irrigation projects include a dam on Vakhsh river, a tributary of the Amu Darya. Mention should be made of the Kara Kum canal which crosses the desert and carries Amu Darya water to the ancient irrigation systems on the Murgheb river. The huge new irrigation system constructed in the Fargana Valley and in

Figure 16
Tajikistan

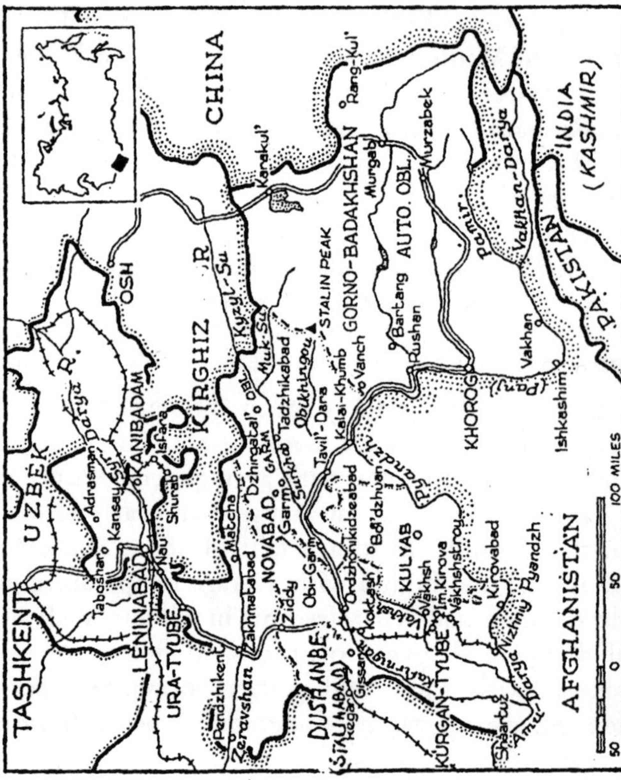

Source: Shabad, Theodore, (1961), *Geography of The USSR*, New York, 381.

the Vakhsh Valley, the Great Gissar Canal, is of great significance in promoting agriculture in Tajikistan. About 75 per cent of the 7 per cent of the arable land of Tajikistan is irrigated.

Agriculture

Tajikistan is an important cotton producer. Formerly, cotton was grown only in the northern Fargana Valley, but now it is grown also in Kafirnigan and Vakhsh valleys. In these valleys the climate is warm and long staple Egyptian cotton is grown here. The area under cotton in these valleys is one-third of the total area under cotton in Tajikistan. The total production of cotton in 2002 was 113,000 metric tonnes.

Among the cereals wheat, rice, barely, maize and millet are cultivated. Table 21 shows the production of principal crops in different years respectively in thousand metric tonnes.

Wheat, barely, rye and some millet are grown in the Leninabed province mainly on the unirrigated areas. Wheat is also cultivated in the Gram province, while in Badakhashan autonomous province wheat is cultivated in the deep valleys in the western portion.

Table 21 shows that the production of wheat has been decreasing over the years and compared to 2000 the production in 2001 decreased marginally in 2001 and 2002. The cultivation of cotton shows great fluctuation. The cultivation of rice has significantly decreased over the years. Around 7 per cent of Tajikistan's land is arable, the remainder being largely mountainous; the economy of the republic is predominantly agricultural. In 2001 and 2002, agriculture contributed 29.3 per cent of the revenue and provided employment to less than half of the population. Agriculture provided employment to 41 per cent of the population, industry 33 per cent, thus three-fourth of the population draw sustenance from agriculture and industry and one-fourth from other occupations like constructions, transport and communication, education and health care. Agriculture is the major activity and after wheat, the cultivation of potatoes is next most important crop, with production of 357,000 metric tonnes. There is substantial production of vegetables and fruits (Table 21).

Table 21
Principal Crops

(in 000 metric tonnes)

Crops	*2000*	*2001*	*2002*
Wheat	406	389	361
Rice	82	40	29
Barley	19	16	15
Maize	38	42	35
Potatoes	303	318	357
Cotton seed	175	190	210
Cabbages	32	36	43
Tomatoes	150	100	202
Onions	110	124	148
Carrots	24	27	32
Other vegetables	38	43	51
Apples	81	73	75
Apricots	32	29	30
Peaches	21	19	18
Plums	14	13	12
Watermelons	95	97	98
Grapes	110	111	100
Other fruits and berries	22	19	11
Cotton lint	93	115	113
Tobacco leaves	07	04	04

Pastures in the upland provide good fodder for livestock which constitute the basis of the economy of eastern provinces. In the mountains of western Tajikistan, the Gissar sheep is raised for meat and fat while in south-western Tajikistan where the climate is relatively hot and dry the Karakul sheep is reared for fur. Some of the dairy cattle are fed on alfalfa. In 2002, the number of sheep in Tajikistan was 1.2 million and the number of cattle was 1.09 million (Table 22 and 23).

Table 22
Livestock

(in 000 herd)

Animals	*2000*	*2001*	*2002*
Horses	72	72	71
Cattle	1037	1052	1001
Camel	43	42	42
Sheep	1472	1478	1490
Goats	706	744	779
Poultry	770	1062	1320

Source: Europa, Vol. II.

Table 23
Livestock Products

(in 000 metric tonnes)

Products	*2000*	*2001*	*2002*
Beef and veal	11.5	14.5	16.5
Mutton, lamb and goat meat	16.0	12.9	14.2
Poultry meat	2.3	1.8	2.1
Cow's milk	309.8	315.6	381.0
Goat's milk	24.3	25.5	31.0
Cheeses	6.5	6.9	6.5
Wool	2.1	2.2	2.1
Wool scoured	1.2	1.3	1.3
Cattle hides (fresh)	1.2	1.6	1.8
Sheep skins (fresh)	2.1	1.7	1.8

Source: Europa, Vol. II.

Mineral and Power Resources

There is a long and impressive list of minerals produced in Tajikistan. Lead, zinc and tungsten are mined in the north-east of Khudzand (Leninabad) of the republic. Coal, oil, sulphur, gold, lead, tin, bauxite and radio-active mineral ore are also mined. The production of coal in 2002 was 27,200 metric tonnes, crude petroleum 16,000 tonnes, natural gas 33 million cu m and copper 16,200 tonnes. Gold production amounted to 27,000 kg in 2002. In late 1993, a new gold mine was discovered in the west of the country which provides 4 metric tonnes of gold per year.[3]

As regards power resources, the deposits of coal as well as petroleum and natural gas are small and Tajikistan has to rely heavily on imports of petroleum and gas. Almost 75 per cent of the domestic electricity requirements are met from hydroelectricity. A new hydroelectric power station was built in 1995 at Rogun. The output of electricity in 2001 was 14,382 million Mkw and gypsum (crude) 55,000 metric tonnes.

Industrial Development

It is only in recent years that industrial development has taken place in Tajikistan. There are not many industries including heavy industry except mineral extraction, aluminum production and power generation. Light industry concentrates on food processing, textiles and carpet making. Its production of cotton yarn was 15,000 tonnes, woven cotton fabric was 14 m sq metres, woven silk fabrics 248,000 sq metres, footwear 100,000 pairs, and cement 69,000 tonnes in 2001. The mining industry is carried on in the north-west in the Fargana Valley and adjacent ranges. The production of wheat flour was 315,000 metric tonnes.

Employment

The total number of people employed in Tajikistan in 2001 was 2,246,000. Of this 1,452,000 or 64 per cent were employed in agriculture, while in construction 31,000 or about 1.30 per cent and in trade and catering 72,000 or 3.2 per cent and transport communication 43,000 or 1.9 per cent in 2001.

Towns

Dushanbe is the capital of Tajikistan. Formerly, the capital was Stalinabad. The total population of Dushanbe in 2004 was 604,694. Other towns in the province are: Kharjand (155,000), Kuboli (83,415), Qurganteppa (60,060), Istravshan (54,304) Kanibadam (47,960), Kofarnihon (48,000), Tierseezare (40,000), Isfara (39,164), Panjakent (34,660) in 2004. Kansay and Taboshee are centres of lead, zinc and uranium in the northern provinces.

Khudzand (Leninabad) is the capital of the province Khuzand. It is situated on the Syr Darya and is important as cotton and silk processing centre. There are a number of industries producing consumer goods.

Stalinabad is the capital of the province Stalinabad and lies south of Khudzand. It lies on the railroad from Kayan and the highway from Khudzand (Leninabad). It has been the political and cultural centre of Tajikistan for a long time and has also been the industrial centre. Cotton and silk mills are located here. It has meat packing and tanning plants. It manufactures hydroelectric turbines, and agricultural implements.

Kurgan-Tyube lies in the Vash Valley. It is a large cotton ginning centre and produces cotton seed oil, meat and flour. It is also the junction of railway lines which radiate from here to various directions.

Kulyab lies in the interfluve of two rivers: Panj and Vakhsh. It is a small town with cotton ginning and metal factories. There is an extensive walnut forest in the north.

Novabad is a new town and is the capital of the Gram province. Formerly the capital was Gram, situated on the Surkhab river. Later on, the capital was transferred to Novabad which means new town. It is situated in a wheat and livestock area.

Khorog is the capital of Badakshan province and is situated on the river Gunt and Panj. Badakshan is an autonomous province, in the Pamir highlands, in the south-east of

Tajikistan. On the east lies China, on the South Afghanistan. There is a sixteen km strip which separates it from Afghanistan-Khorog is situated on the highway from Kyrgyzstan which runs south and skirts the Karakul lake and then turns west and joins Khorog and then runs for some distance close to Panj river and then it turns to north-west, joins Stalinabad and then turns to north and meets Khudzand and Tashkent.

Trade

Exports

The total exports from Tajikistan was 538 million US dollars in 2001. About 73.8 per cent of the export consisted of mineral product and base metal (aluminum) worth 397 million dollars and the remaining 27 per cent of the export consisted of textile worth about (62) and electricity (79) million dollars.

Imports

Tajikistan imports considerable amount of mineral products. Its total value of import was about 547 million dollars in 2002 out of the total import 43.3 per cent (184 million US dollars) consisted of mineral products (alumina) in 2001. Of the remaining 57 per cent of imports consists of natural gas (27 million), petroleum products (78 million), electricity (98 million) and grain and flour (38 million).

Trading Partners

Exports (2002)

The major trading partners of Tajikistan in respect of exports were Hungary, Russia, Switzerland and Turkey which accounted for about 80 per cent (266 million dollars of the total exports of 335 million dollars). The remaining 20 per cent of the exports went to six countries namely Iran, Italy, Belgium, Latvia, Netherlands and Uzbekistan (Table 24).

Table 24
Principal Trading Partners

(in US million dollars)

Export	*2000*	*2001*	*2002*
Belgium	5.1	6.0	5.0
Hungary	1.0	38.8	65.8
Iran	12.5	29.9	24.8
Italy	21.4	5.8	18.9
Latvia	-	11.7	12.7
Netherlands	178.2	194.4	2.8
Russia	258.8	104.7	64.4
Switzerland	72.2	52.2	54.1
Turkey	58.4	75.1	81.5
Uzbekistan	97.8	87..2	4.7

Table 25
Principal Trading Partners

(in US million dollars)

Import	*2000*	*2001*	*2002*	*%*
Azerbaijan	63.1	33.5	36.4	6.6
Iran	7.6	10	10.6	2.0
Kazakhstan	82.4	89.1	96.7	17.6
Rumania	41.0	10.9	11.8	2.1
Russia	105.1	129.4	88.0	16.0
Switzerland	0.6	2.1	2.1	0.50
Turkistan	29.3	62.3	67.6	12.3
Ukraine	-	63.6	69.0	12.6
U.K	86.9	2.5	1.2	0.21
Uzbekistan	185.6	150.7	163.6	30.0
Total			547	

Imports (2002)

In respect of imports, Tajikistan got about 30 per cent of the value of imports (163.6 million US dollars) from Uzbekistan, about 16.0 per cent from Russia about 17.6 per cent from Kazakhstan of the remaining 36 per cent of the imports came from Ukraine, Azerbaijan and Turkmenistan (Table 25).

Notes

1. *Europa World Year Book 1998,* Vol. II p. 3267
2. ESCAP population data sheet 2004.
3. *Europa World Year Book 2004,* Vol. II p. 4085.

6

Kyrgyzstan

The Republic of Kyrgyzstan is a small state in the eastern part of Central Asia surrounded by land on all sides. The country is also known as Kyrgyzia. Kyrgyzstan shares its borders with the Republic of Kazakhstan in the north, the Republic of Uzbekistan in the west, Tajikistan in the south, and People's Republic of China in the east. Its total area is 198,500 sq km and its total population in 2004 was 5,208,000.[1]

Historical Background

The ancestors of Kyrgyz were settled in the upper reaches of the Yenisei river until about the tenth century AD. From there they migrated to the Tien Shan region owing to the rise of Mongol empire in the 13th century. Later on, they became part of the Russian Empire by 1919 and until 1924, it was a part of Turkestan in the Soviet Union. In 1925, it was renamed Kyrgyz Autonomous oblast, and in 1926 it became an autonomous Kyrgyz Republic of Soviet Union. The Republic adopted a declaration of sovereignty in 1990 and in September 1991 it became an independent sovereign democratic state and a member of the CIS in December 1991. The head of the state is Askar Akayev elected on 24 December 1995 for a period of five years. He was re-elected President of Republic on 29 October 2000 for a period of five years. Majority of the people follow Islam but the declared policy of the State is secularism.

Topography

Kyrgyzstan is a land of high mountains and plateau. Most of the territory is taken up by the mountains of Tein Shan ranges, the foot of which has rich grazing grounds. On the borders of China, the mountains rise to about 8,000 m above sea level and are the sources of many rivers of Central Asia and Western China.

There are two sections where the topography is characterized by lowlands. In the north are the valleys of Chu and the Talas rivers while the eastern part of the Fergana Valley falls in the Khirghi territory. The lowlands lie at an elevation of 400 to 500 m above sea level and constitute good agricultural lands. Similarly, the basin of lake Issyk-Kul situated on a high plateau and surrounded by mountain ranges is suitable for agricultural purposes. The main mass of this plateau is 200 km wide and consists of broad basins about 3,000 m above the sea level in an east-west direction. Two important rivers rise from this plateau. The Chu flows to the north in a deep cleft and then turns to the north-east and for about 150 km forms the boundary between Kyrgyzstan and Kazakhstan. The Naryn river, a right bank tributary of Syr Darya flows westward and enters the Fergana valley north of the Fergana range (Figure 17).

Eastern Kyrgyzstan is lower than the western Kyrgyzstan and has U-shaped opening to the west and embraces the Fergana valley from the north and south. The Syr Darya in this region is called Kara Darya which rises in the south-west of Kyrgyzstan (Figure 17).

Figure 17
Kyrgyzstan

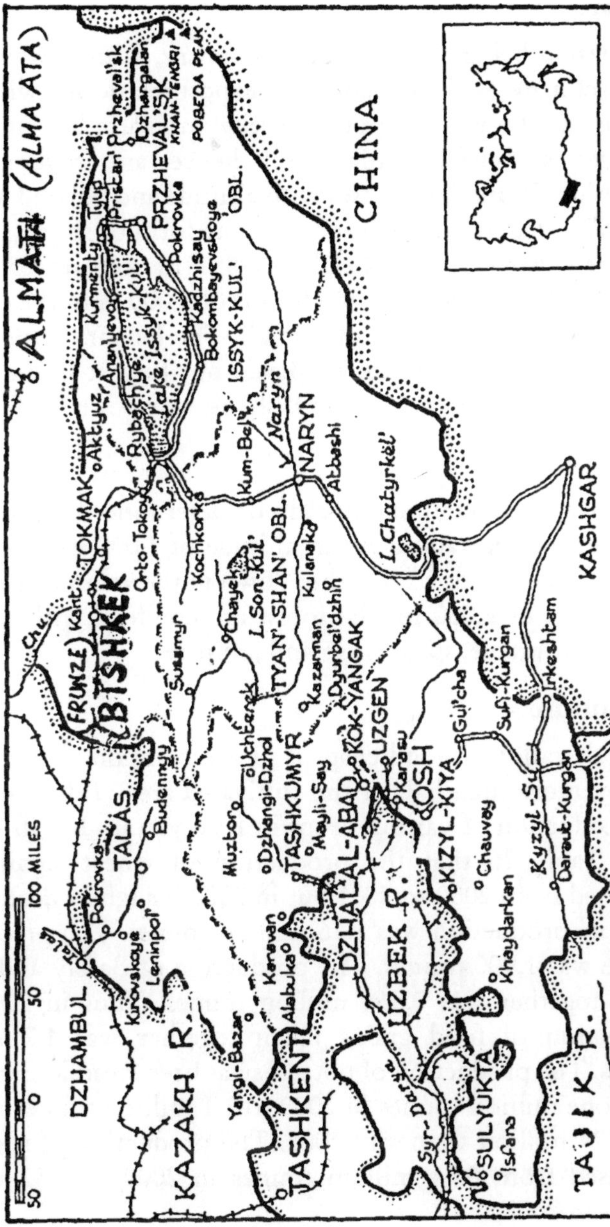

Source: Shabad Theodore (1961), *Geography of the USSR*, New York, p. 373.

Climate

Kyrgyzstan being a mountainous country, witnesses variation in its climate with altitude and exposure; slopes which are exposed to the west or north, receive moisture bearing winds and get sufficient rainfall and hence are covered with vegetation. Rainfall increases with altitude and beyond a height of 3,000-4,000 m precipitation is in the form of snow. Bishkek (formerly Frunze) at a height of 850 m receives 35 cm of rainfall, while Przhevalsk at a height of 2,000 m in the extreme north-east receives 45 cm of rainfall. The January temperature is below freezing at both the places but July at Przhevalsk is cooler (18°-19°C) compared to Bishkek where it is 25°C.

Vegetation

Exposure, precipitation and altitude determine the nature and thickness of vegetation. At an altitude of 4,000 m, one comes across alpine meadows. Further down in the valley bottom and at a height of 2,000 m, the forest are conifers, with varieties such as fir, maple, spruce, ash and juniper.

Agriculture

The cultivation of food crops is of great importance and they occupy more than half of the cultivated area. Table 26 shows the production of various crops in Kyrgyzstan. It will be seen from Table 26 that the production of wheat significantly increased from 2000 to 2001 but in 2002 it slightly declined. In 2002, its production was 1.16 million tonnes. The production of rice was 1,900 tonnes. The production of Barely and Miaze taken together was 0.564 million tonnes. Thus in 2002, the production of food grains taken together was 1.7 million tonnes. The production of potatoes has been steadily increasing from one million tonnes in 2000 to 1.1 million tonnes in 2001 and 1.24 million tonnes in 2002. The production of sugarbeet increased from 0.44 million tonnes in 2000 to 0.52 million tonnes in 2002.

There is a large variety of vegetables and fruits which Krygyzstan grows: cabbage, tomato, cucumber, carrot, onion and other vegetables and the production of all the vegetables taken together was 0.189 million tonnes. The production of a variety of fruits including water melons in 2002 was 0.241 million tonnes (Table 26).

Table 26

Agriculture: Principal Crops

(in 000 metric tonnes)

Crops	*2000*	*2001*	*2002*
Wheat	1039.1	1190.6	1103.0
Rice	-	-	6.5
Barely	150.2	139.9	165.9
Maize	338.3	442.8	428.2
Potato	1045.6	1168.4	1240.0
Sugarbeet	449.8	286.6	524.5
Cabbage	100.5	119.1	130.1
Tomatoes	155.6	165.5	183.5
Cucumber	124.0	162.1	170.0
Onions	147.4	149.2	131.9
Carrots	109.4	112.5	126.7
Other vegetables	109.9	105.0	76.3
Apple	127.9	126.3	115.2
Apricot	16.7	16.5	14.9
Peach	6.4	8.0	10.0
Grape	26.5	27.4	17.7
Watermelon	67.1	85.5	83.0
Cotton lint	28.7	33.7	46.0

Among the non-food grain crops, cotton is most important. It is largely grown in the Fergana Valley. Most of the irrigated lands lie in the Chu Valley, Talas river valley in Fergana and in the valley of Issyk-Kul.

The Chu Valley is the most important centre for the cultivation of fiberous crops such as hemp and jute. Other crops that are cultivated are sugarbeet, tobacco, poppy seed in the valley of Talas and in the basin of Issyk-Kul.

Livestock raising occupies a very important place in the economy of Kyrgyzstan. In the mountain zone about 10 to 12 million hectares are suitable for pasture lands. The people in the valleys practice transhumance. In the spring season in the valleys and mountain slopes, there is rich luxuriant vegetation and the people along with their herds migrate to the higher levels and stay there throughout the summers. The cattle population was about 1 million in 2002, that of sheep about 3.1 million and goats 0.64 million, while the number of poultry was 3.25 million (2002). The extensive grazing grounds provide a stable and abundant supply of forage. The mountain slopes are covered with rich grasslands. The meadows contain patches of sparse willow and birch. Further up, among the forests of fir trees, valuable grazing grounds are also found. Still further up the mountain, there are alpine pastures as a result Kyrgyzstan in 2002 produced about 1.1 million tonnes of milk, 14,000 tonnes of butter, 4,860 thousand tonnes of cheese and 1,36,000 tonnes of various type of meat[2]. Apart from dairy products it produced about 18 thousand tonnes of wool.

Mineral Resources

Kyrgyzstan compared to other Central Asian states has better resources of coal. The chief mines are at the margin of Fergana Valley; at Sulyukta and Kizyl-Kiya. Both the sites are along the southern projection of Uzbekistan bordering Kyrgyzstan. The other sites are at Kok-Yangak and Tashkumyr, the former is located near the extreme eastern projection of Uzbekistan, while the latter is on the northern border of this projection. There are some minor deposits at Kadzhisay at the southern shore of Issyk-Kul lake. Coaking coal is mined to the east of Uzgen along the Yassy river; other mines are Dzhargalan which is to the north of Przhevalsk, in the east of lake

Issyk-Kul. Kizyl Kiya along the southern border of the lake. In 2000-03, total production of coal was 411,000 metric tonnes.

Petroleum wells are located in the eastern Feragna Valley at Changyrtash and Maylsay. In 2003, 69,000 tonnes of oil were produced and the output of natural gas was 27.1 million cubic metre.

Kyrgyzstan is endowed with rich mineral resources such as lead, zinc, mercury and tungsten. On the southern edge of the Fergana Valley there are abundant deposits of mercury and antimony in Khaydarkan, Bishkek and Chauvay. There is a lead mine with a mixture of tin ore at Aktyuz situated in the north of lake Issuk-Kul. Sulphur is quarried at Changyrtash. There are well developed arsenic deposits at Uchimchak in the mountains south west of Talas. Uranium is mined at Tyuya-Muyun and at Maylgsay.

Industrial Development

Kyrgyzstan specializes in agro-industries. The chief industries are based on local agricultural products such as sugarbeet, tobacco, milk and meat. Cotton ginning plants are concentrated in Fergana Valley. Excluding tobacco, all industries are situated around Bishkek. Textile fabrics of the order of 5.5 million sq metre (in 2003) footwear 171,000 pairs cement 0.53 million tonnes, electrical energy 12 thousands kwh.[1] Cigarettes 2,927 million and refined sugar 51,000 tonnes, vegetables oil 11 thousand metric tonnes were produced in 2003.

Population

The total population of Kyrgyzstan in 2004 was 5,208,000 with an average density of 26 persons per sq km. The main ethnic groups can be seen from Table 5.

The growth rate of population is 3.4 per cent per annum. The total population employed in Kyrgyzstan was 1,764,000. The total number of people employed in agriculture and forestry was 923,000, in manufacturing and construction, 172,000, in transport 66,000. However, the number of total employed persons in the Republic is small. It was 1,764,000 or about one-third of the total population.

Towns

Bishkek (formerly Frunze) is the capital of Kyrgyzstan. It is located in the centre of Chu Valley at the foot of Kirghis range. The town lies in the north of Kyrgyzstan on the branch railway which connects Bishkek with some towns of Kazakhstan like Dzhambul. The city was built in 1873 and was named Pishpek. In 1925, it was renamed after the Bolshevik General M.V. Frunze born there in 1885. It was renamed as Bishkek after independence.

Chu Valley in which it is located is known as sugar valley, as it produces sugarbeet and there are more then five large sugar mills in the valley. The valley has a large number of hydroelectric power stations. The main crops cultivated in the valley are fibre crops and sugarbeet. The Bishkek and the second city Tokmak, specialize in fruits and vegetables. Apart from the production of vegetables on a large scale in the neighbourhood of Bishkek, there are light manufacturing industries like meat packaging, flour milling, fruit canning, fibre processing, textiles processing, shoe manufacturing and tobacco processing.

Tomak is situated at a distance of about of 50 km from Bishkek. It has a sugar refinery, an auto repair plant and is also engaged in the processing of fibre crops.

Przhevalsk is the capital of the province of Issuk-Kul. It is a transit point leading to the Kazakh Republic. It is also a junction where the roads skirting all round the Issuk-Kul meet at Rybac'ye and another road runs south up to Kashgar in Afghanistan. Naryn is the capital of the province of Tyan Shan. It is a small town of 30,000 people on the Naryn river and serves as a trading centre as well.

Osh

The city is situated in southern Kyrgyzstan, close to the eastern projected end of Uzbekistan. Osh has been an important silk centre since the eighth century and specializes in textile industry. A number of silk spinning mills are also found here. Cotton textile, food processing and tobacco manufacturing are some of the other important industries. Close by is a health resort and a rock named Solomon's throne known for attracting pilgrims.

In the south-west of Kyrgyzstan in the Osh province, about 60 km west lies the town Kizyl Kiya and 200 km in the extreme south-west lies the town of Sulyukta. Both the towns are mining centres.

Dzhalal-Abad is the capital of the province of Dzhalal Abad. It is a big town having a developed manufacturing industry. It is situated in the extreme east in the north of the pincers around the Fergana Valley of Uzbekistan. It has textile mills, food processing plants, metal and tobacco industries. Nearly the entire slopes of the Fergana range is covered with nut and almond trees, including fruit trees of apples, plums and apricots. Dzhalal-Abad has a large vitamin and canning plant based on the abundant availability of fruits and nuts.

Kok-Yangak situated close to Dzhalal-Abad and Tashkumyr, about 150 km to the north west of Dzhalal-Abad are the two major coal mining centres. Talas lies on the river Talas to the north of the province of Talas. Economically it is linked with Dzhamabul of Kazakhstan. In the valley of Talas, tobacco, flax and wheat are grown and the mountain slopes provide ample grazing ground for the cattle population.

Transport and Means of Communication

The transport system of Kyrgyzstan can be divided into two parts: the railways and the roadways.

The railway system is common in the northern lowland of Chu Valley. There is a railway which runs from Kazakhstan to

Chu Valley through Bishkek, the capital of Kyrgyzstan and Tokmak to Rubachye, a port on the western end of the lake Issyk Kul.

Roadways skirt the lake Issyk-Kul all round. The road system that has been constructed around the lake is very important since wheat is cultivated along the eastern shore of the lake, and a cement plant is located on the northern shore. Then there are food processing industries along the eastern shore. Again, the mountain surrounding the lake contain many health resorts. A road system runs from the western end of the lake and goes further south and crossing the southern boundary of Kyrgyzstan goes on to Kashgar. Another route from Kizyl-Kiya runs southwards near the southern boundary, a trunk road branches off to Kashyar.

Trade

Exports

There are seventeen countries to which Kyrgyzstan exported its goods in 2003; out of these, two countries, namely, UAE (about 27 per cent) and Switzerland (about 22 per cent), – about half of the total export of Kyrgyzstan were the recipients. Russia and three Central Asian reputes (Kazakhstan, Tajikistan and Uzbekistan) received 36 per cent of the total exports. Thus, six countries taken together received about 85 per cent of the total exports and China and Turkey together share 7 per cent of the exports. Thus, eight countries received 92 per cent of total exports out of 17 countries (Table 27).

Imports

In respect of imports in 2003 by Kyrgyzstan, five countries namely Russia, two central Asian countries Kazakhstan and Uzbekistan; and China and Germany shared 80 per cent of the imports and if Turkey and USA are added, the total imports from the countries would go up to 91 per cent, thus out of the 20 countries seven countries sent 91 per cent of the imports of Kyrgyzstan (Table 28).

Table 27
Principal Trading Partners

(in US million dollar)

Exports	*2001*	*2002*	*2003*
Afghanistan	1.6	4.4	6.1
Azerbaijan	2.1	5.6	2.0
People's Republic of China	19.4	41.1	23.3
France	1.8	5.6	0.2
Germany	94.4	1.8	3.0
India	1.4	6.1	0.7
Iran	8.2	4.7	2.1
Kazakhstan	39.0	36.8	57.1
Latvia	3.4	8.7	9.4
Russia	64.5	80.4	97.0
Switzerland	124.2	96.4	117.9
Tajikistan	6.7	10.2	18.9
Turkey	13.8	16.4	11.0
UAE	0.5	68.8	144.3
UK	14.1	0.9	0.1
USA	7.1	36.1	6.5
Uzbekistan	48.0	27.8	16.3
Total			515.9

Table 28
Principal Trading Partners

(in US million dollar)

Imports	*2001*	*2002*	*2003*
Belarus	6.0	5.1	5.9
Belgium	8.4	1.6	3.3
Canada	1.9	9.0	8.3
People's Republic of China	48.5	59.1	77.7
Germany	24.3	31.4	38.2
Iran	6.7	4.3	5.9

Contd...

Contd...

Japan	5.8	6.4	11.8
Kazakhstan	81.8	123.9	170.9
Korea	7.8	7.0	11.7
Netherlands	4.0	16.1	12.3
Poland	4.9	3.9	6.1
Russia	55.1	116.7	176.1
Sweden	0.9	7.4	2.0
Turkey	15.8	17.0	26.0
Turkmenistan	9.0	1.7	0.4
Ukraine	6.2	7.8	12.6
UAE	6.8	7.3	7.8
UK	4.8	2.8	2.5
Uzbekistan	66.7	60.1	39.2
USA	26.8	47.4	47.9
Total			665.6

Notes

1. Data obtained from ESCAP Population Data Sheet, 2004.
2. Data obtained from *Europa*, *World Year Book 1998*, Vol. II, p. 2032.
3. *Europe World Year Book 2004*, Vol. II, p. 2032.

7

Kazakhstan

Kazakhstan is the biggest state in Central Asia and its area is greater then the combined area of the remaining four states: Turkmenistan, Uzbekistan, Tajikistan and Kyrgyzstan. The area of Kazakhstan is 2,717,300 sq km. The combined area of the four states is 1,236,400 sq km which is 45 per cent of the area of Kazakhstan.

The Republic extends 1,900 km from the Volga river in the west to the Altai mountains in the east, and about 1,300 km from the northern boundary of Trans-Siberian railway in the Siberian plain to the Central Asian deserts, in the south. Its latitudinal extent is 40° to 55.5° N latitude and 45°–85°E longitude. Kazakhstan is bordered in the south by Turkmenistan, Uzbekistan and Kyrgyzstan. In the east it is bordered by the People's Republic of China. In the north the border coincides with the Russian Federation and in the south-west the boundary consists of coast line of 2,320 km on the Caspian Sea (Figure 18). Its population in 2004 was 15,403,000.[1]

Figure 18
Kazakhstan

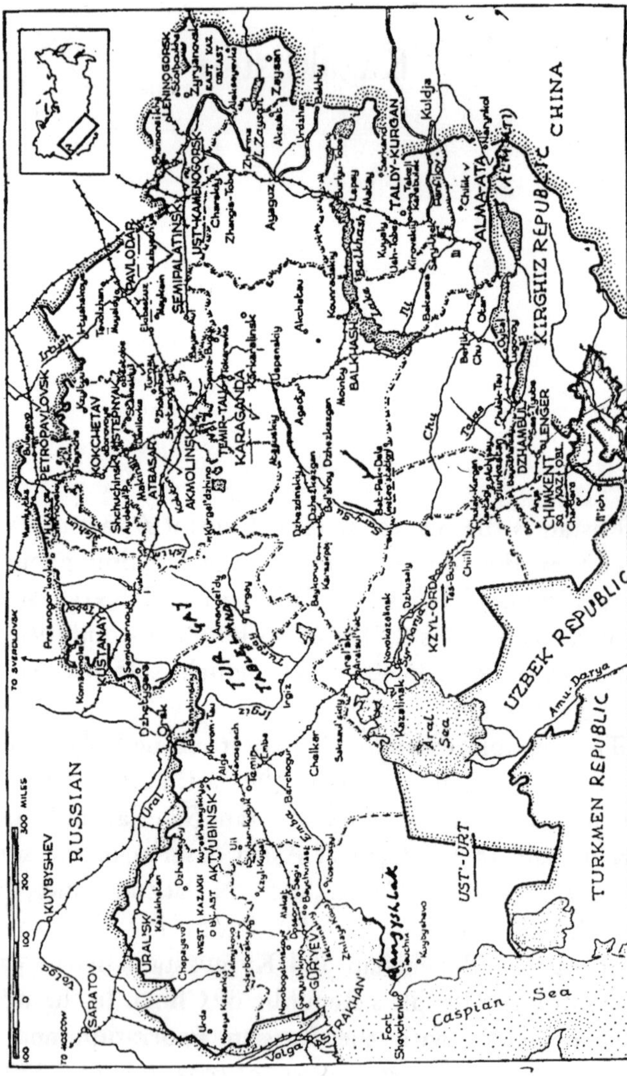

Source: Shabad, Theodore (1961), *Geography of the USSR*, New York, pp. 338-339.

Historical Background

In view of Kazakhstan's very large size, its potential resources and the state being the fourth nuclear power in the world, a detailed historical account of the state is given below.

The Kazakhs are descendants of Mongols and Turkie tribes that settled in the area in the first century BC and were a known distinct ethnic group as Kazakh Orda which was formed in the late 15th century AD.

In the early 17th century, Kazakh Orda was dissolved and three large groups came into existence. The Mongols invaded the three hordes (federation) which asked for protection from the Russian Tsar. Although the threat later on ended, the Russians retained their control over the Kazakhs and many Russian and Ukrainian peasants who moved to Kazakhstan were granted Kazakh lands. There was resentment against the Russian rule and in 1916 a major rebellion broke out which was suppressed, although 150,000 people were killed.[2]

Gorbachev's accession to power in 1985, led to public debate on environmental and linguistic issues and in 1989, Kazakh recognized as the official language of Kazakhstan while Russian remained a language of inter-ethnic communication. In 1991 it was announced that nuclear testing would not continue in eastern Kazakhstan.

It was in 1989, that Nursultan Nazarbayev, an ethnic Kazakh who had been Chairman of the council of Ministers of the Republic since March 1984, was elected President of Kazakhstan and on the 16 December, 1991, Kazakhstan declared its independence from USSR. The country's name was changed as the Republic of Kazakhstan. On December 1, 1991, Nursultan Nazarbayev was elected President securing 98.8 per cent votes for a period of five years and in December 1996 he was elected President up to December 2001. Nursultan A. Nazarbayev continues to be the President of the state and was re-elected in January 1999.

Nursultan's effort to preserve racial harmony and democratic principles have been widely acclaimed internationally. Kazakhstan also became a member of the CIS.

Topography

Kazakhstan is a vast flat land, lowest in the west and highest in the east. In the south-east there is a high mountain which forms its boundary. In the west lies the Caspian depression, the higher upland and the Bet Pak Dala in the centre, and the Altay and Tein Shan mountain in the east and south-east.

Kazakhstan's physical landscape can be better understood by dividing it into three natural regions: (1) Western Region with the low Caspian depression and Turan lowland in the west and the south-west, (2) Central Region consisting of higher Kazakh upland including Bet-Pak Dala, and (3) the Eastern Region with Altay and Tein Shan mountain belt.

Western Region

The western region comprises the Caspian depression and the Turan lowland. This is a region of subsidence. There are many areas on the shore of the Caspian sea which are 30 metres below sea level. The plain ends abruptly against the Mangyshlak peninsula in the Kara Tau or Black mountain which is a fault block plateau with a valley that runs the entire length of the peninsula. In the south-eastern part of the peninsula the elevation varies from about 600 m above sea level to about 150 m below sea level. However, this area today serves as a mining region for oil, manganese and phosphates. In the east of Caspian Sea lies the Ust-Urt plateau which is dry and barren. It has cliff like escarpment called '*chink*'. The whole landscape of this plateau is one of the most desolate desert (Figure 18).

The Aral Sea lies in the middle section of the Turanian low-land. The Aral Sea is the fourth largest lake in the world with a surface area of almost 65,000 sq km. It is a shallow sea with depth of only 10 to 20 metres. Aral Sea contains thousands of islands. The name Aral means 'island sea'. The two rivers,

Syr Darya and Amu Darya which drain into Aral Sea, have built deltas near their mouths in the north-east and in the southern side. A few thousand years ago, the Aral Sea drained southwestward into the Caspian. The average salt content of Aral Sea is less than 1 per cent compared to Caspian Sea where, in the south-eastern part, the salt content is about 14 per cent. Precipitation in this region is scanty, less then 10 cm per annum. The Aral Sea owes its existence to the water of the rivers, the Syr Darya and the Amu Darya, which are fed by the snowclad mountain in the south-east and the fractured aquifers. Owing to the massive irrigation by canals taken out from the rivers, the supply of water in the Aral Sea has dwindled and the sea has shown signs of much shrinkage. The water of the lake is very clear and the bottom can be seen even at a depth of 20 metres.

North of Aral Sea the desert presents a desolate appearance and there are ridges of sand dunes oriented south-southwest, north-northeast. These sands dunes are known as *Great Barsuki* in the north-west of Aral sea, and as *Small Barsuki* in the north of the Aral sea. The remote empty desert called Turgary Tableland provides ideal sites for ICBM bases. South of the Aral Sea the Turanian lowlands project into the western parts of the Kara-Kum or black sands desert to the foothills of the Kopet Dag up to the Iranian border.[3]

Lying astride is the lowest Syr Darya red sand desert known as Kyzyl Kum, one of the most arid regions of Kazakhstan, to the east of the Aral Sea. The Kyzyl Kum is in fact a rocky desert and in the central and eastern portions rock formations are as high as 1,000 metres. It is a very dry desert. Extending north-westward from the Tien Shan mountain is Karka Tau or the Black mountain overlooking the Muyum Kum or sandy desert bordered on the west and the east by Talas and Chu rivers respectively. These rivers rising from Tien Shan in the south and flowing north-westward, disappear in the desert. The Chu valley separates Muyum Kum, the sandy desert in the south, from Bet Pak Dala to the north.

Bet Pak Dala means a 'tyrant' or crafty steppe. It derives its name from the fact that it deceives a tired traveller by its various mirages. Bet Pak Dala is a dry plateau desert with an elevation of about 150 metres in the south to about 500 metres to the north of lake Balkhash. In the north-west of Bet Pak Dala flows Sary-su river. Bet Pak Dala is also called Hungry Steppe. It has salt encrusted surface and cracked clay with very sparse vegetation and little prospects for development. The Hungry Steppe should not be confused with the Hungry Steppe south-west of Tashkent in Uzbekistan where irrigation has converted large areas into smiling cotton fields south-west of Syr Darya (Figure 18).

Eastern Section

Lake Balkhash is about 560 km long and lies at an elevation of about 400 metres above sea level and covers an area of 17,000 sq km with an average depth of about seven metres. The salt content of the lake is very low which shows that it is of recent origin. The river rising from Tein Shan falls in the lake in its western end and its water could be used for irrigation and drinking purposes. The lake in the western portion is less saltish owing to the discharge of the river Ili, but in the eastern section it is much saltish due to high evaporation. The lake seems to be in the process of drying up and becoming more salty. A sand bar practically divides the lake into two parts – the fresh body of water in the west from the salty water in the east (Figure 18).

Drainage

All rivers of Kazakhstan except Irtysh, drain into inland basin. Rivers like the Chu, the Sary-Su, and the Talas are not useful for irrigation. The Emba, discharges into the Caspian Sea while the river of the Turgay tableland, e.g., the Turgay flows into Irgiz which in turn flows into a salt lake (Figure 18). All these rivers have few tributaries. However, in the spring when the snow melts they are turbulent, but during the summer, they become streaks of water and even dry up in the lower reaches. Among the rivers mentioned, Ural is suitable for irrigation.

In the south and south-east of Kazakhstan, the rivers which have their origin in Tein Shan mountain and the Altay system, are fed by glaciers. Syr Darya, with its tributaries Chirchik and the Arys, discharges its waters into the Aral Sea. The Talas and the Chu in southern Kazakhstan and the Ili, the Karatal, the Ak-Su and the Lepsa, all rising from the eastern mountain, are fed by glaciers and drain into lake Balkhash, and the Irtysh, with its many right hand tributaries, rises in the Altay mountains. These mountain rivers are useful to Kazakhstan in two ways - the upper course of these rivers consists of narrow precipitous valleys and are suitable for the establishment of hydroelectric power stations and in the lower reaches they are used for irrigation. Their usefulness is further enhanced by their regular flow during the year in contrast to the streams in the steppes. The mountain rivers owe their origin to the melting of snow and secondly they have maximum volume at a time, (July-August), when they are most needed for irrigation of the areas under cultivation. The Irtish is suitable for navigation. This river rises in Sinking province of China and is known as Kara Irtysh, and passes through a lake Zaysan 100 km inside the territory of Kazakhstan and the river is navigable for about seven months as it freezes from November to middle of April (Figure 18).

Climate

Kazakhstan's climate is highly continental, but it varies considerably from north to south and from west to east. There are wide variation in the climate. Average temperature in January ranges from –18°C in the north of Kazakhstan to –3°C in the south. The average January temperature everywhere is below freezing except in some isolated areas in the south. The average monthly temperature in January decreases at the same rate degree of 0.3°C for every longitude from west to east[4] along the same degree of latitude. The climate of northern Kazakhstan resembles to that of western Siberia. Winters in northern Kazakhstan are long and hard and summers are short and relatively cool. Rainfall precipitation is scanty in Kazakhstan. In winters there is a cold dry air mass, of arctic origin which covers northern and eastern Kazakhstan. Tropical air centred over Iran sometimes makes inroads in the north and there is some precipitation to the tunes of 5 to 7 cm from November to March and the snow cover in western Kazakhstan is very thin and varies from 30 cm in the north to 5 to 10 cm in the Aral Sea region and further south near the Syr Darya there is no snow at all.

As the season advances, Kazakhstan begins to warm up from April to October. The rainfall in the northern Kazakhstan is about 25 cm, but in central Kazakhstan, the relative humidity in May and June is extremely low, the Aral-Balkhash area receives not more than 3 to 7 cm of rainfall. The mountain ranges in the east receive much greater amount of rainfall. The northernmost range in Altay system receives 30 to 40 cm in winter and 70 to 80 cm in summer. Dzungarian Ala Tau which lies in the same latitude as the Aral Balkhash area has an annual rainfall of 45 cm.

It should be noted that rainfall in Kazakhstan decreases from north to south, but temperature increase from north to south. So decrease in the rainfall and increase in temperature are conditions which lead to desiccation and promote the formation of deserts. The absences of relief and trees promote the free movement of wind and the winds in winter blow at the rate of 20 km per hour. The blowing of wind with such velocity leads to evaporation as well as soil erosion.

Kazakhstan's climate is marked by continentality: summers are long and hot, winters are severe and cold. During the summer months, the diurnal range of temperature is high – in the day time the temperature reaches 38°C or 40°C but in the night it is a few degrees above freezing. Winters are not free from frosts. In the north, frosty nights are common and temperature may go much below the freezing point while in the south it may be near freezing.

Vegetation and Soils

Kazakhstan's vegetation can be best considered in terms of low-lands and uplands. In the uplands, the character of vegetation depends on altitude. Along the foothills the vegetation belongs to the steppe zone, and higher up lies the forested zone and further up the alpine meadows. In the lowland rainfall, more than temperature, determines the character of vegetation, which passes from steppes to semi-desert and finally to desert.

Northern Kazakhstan whose climate resembles western Siberia, has a narrow belt of wooded steppes. The trees are clusters of birch and willows interspersed with pastures supported by black soil. Towards the south, the humus content decreases and the clusters of birch and willows disappear and typical steppes are predominant. The black soil is replaced by chestnut brown soil.

48°N latitude marks the transition from steppes to semi-desert. The chestnut brown soil is replaced by brown semi-desert soil with almost no humus content. The soil has a higher salt content and in the depression it is saline and alkaline. During the spring month, the whole steppe assumes a flowery appearance, but is short-lived and it returns to the brownish colour in the summer.

The deserts in Kazakhstan may be divided into four types: sandy, rocky/stony, clay desert, and salt desert. Turan low-lands present the example of sandy desert and are characterized by numerous longitudinal and crescentic sand dunes. Wherever on these dunes, vegetation has gown, the dunes have been stabilized otherwise they are migratory.

Where stony gravel or debris, as a result of the remains of former mountains, has accumulated, the area has a semblance of rocky or stony desert.

Bet-Pak Dala is a clay desert. During the spring, when there is some rainfall, the area becomes muddy and sticky and it is impossible to cross it, but during the summer the soil becomes very stiff and fissures are formed at places.

Salt desert occur in the low-lying areas and in depressions where water collects during the spring and evaporates in the summer and leaves behind an encrustation of salts.

Kazakhstan is, broadly speaking, a country of treeless plains and the steppe grass supports a very large number of cattle. However, along the streams like Chu, Talas or Emba, thick bushes and cluster of trees are found producing a great contrast to the neighbouring steppe lands. Whenever, the streams are in floods, these sections of river valleys containing the bushes and forests are also inundated. These forest lands in the local language are called *Tugay*. The mountains in the south and south-east are well-forested.

Irrigation

Irrigation works in Kazakhstan are mostly confined to the region surrounding the lower reaches of Syr Darya, region surrounding Almaty (Alma Ata) and Tadly-Kurgan region (Figure 18). The Chu river, a tributary of the Syr Darya, is also utilized for irrigation. The irrigated region around Taldy-Kurgan in the eastern Kazakhstan, south of eastern end of the lake Balkhash, is important for cereal production. It may be mentioned that the Chu river is a feeder of Syr Darya and is used extensively for irrigation in areas surrounding Almaty (Alma Ata) and Kurgan.

Conservation of water for irrigation is the greatest need in Kazakhstan. There is a lot of wastage of water in the process of irrigation owing to inefficient technique. Water is lost by evaporation and the accumulation of salts leads to salinity in the soil. Water is also lost from canals through seepage, as all the canals are not lined. Kazakhstan needs to introduce sprinkler irrigation on a large scale. This will economize the use of water in irrigation. In sprinkler irrigation, water is sprayed on the land from a rotating tube on a point and irrigates a circular area with a radius of half a km. Kazakhstan has taken steps in this direction in the Tenth Five-Year Plan (1975-1980).

Considerable areas of Kazakhstan are desert. Irrigation, while a boon in converting large areas into smiling fields and produce food grains and industrial crops for the benefit of people, also brings about a permanent damage to the land, if water is not used judiciously. When the land is covered by water owing to excessive irrigation the water table rises as surplus water seeps downwards. Seepage also takes place if the canals are unlined. Water with dissolved salts percolates into the subsoil and makes the subsoil water highly saline and during intense heat in the summers months, as a result of capillary action, the solution with dissolved salt comes to the surface, the water evaporates, leaving behind salt efflorescence on the surface. The land thus gets impregnated with salt.

Excessive use of water also leads to waterlogging. Waterlogging does not only mean that the area is covered with water. An area is said to be waterlogged when the water table rises to an extent that the soil pores in the root zone of a crop become saturated resulting in restriction of the normal circulation of air, and a decline in the level of oxygen and an increase in the level of carbon dioxide takes place. The level of water table which is considered harmful would depend upon the type of crop, type of soil and the quality of water. The actual depth of water table, when it starts affecting the yield of the crop adversely, may vary over a wide range from zero for rice to about 1.5 metre for other crops. Wheat is affected when the water table is within 0.6 metre, maize, millet and cotton are sensitive to water table within 1.2 metre and barley within 0.9 metre.

Thus, in irrigated areas it is desirable to keep the average water table well beyond the capillary range, around 5 metres, if not deeper. Apart from the risk of increasing soil salinity, a high water table is wasteful for groundwater resources as it contributes to unproductive evaporation. Also a low water table provides more space for groundwater recharge during the rainy season and thus helps in increasing the groundwater resource.[5]

In southern Kazakhstan irrigation is widely practised and the ground water reserves, which are extensive, can be utilized judiciously. Kazakhstan has ground water reserves estimated at 5,000 km^3 in the southern part of the Republic, but the use has not been greater than 2.5 thousand km^3.[6]

Drawing of excessive water for irrigation both from Syr Darya and Amu Darya has led to worry in respect of the future of Aral Sea. The level of Aral Sea was relatively stable from 1911 until 1960, but dropped by nearly 3 metres by 1975. Further extensive withdrawal from the rivers for irrigation has reduced sea level to the tune of 8 to 10 metres by 2000 AD. leading to a shrinkage of the sea by one quarter of its size. Fish catches have declined by 50 per cent as a consequence of increasing salinity. The eventual conversion of the sea into a residual brine lake, as more and more water is drawn from the rivers, is very likely. This is likely to reduce precipitation and salt deposits from the drier margins may be blown to adjacent agriculturally productive land.[7]

It may be mentioned that eastern and south-eastern parts of Kazakhstan posses extensive water courses and the streams form part of the inland drainage system of the Aral Sea and the Caspian Sea and the lakes Balkhash and Tengiz, the major exception being the rivers Irtysh, Tobol and the Ishim. Irtish drains into the river Ob and the river Tobol joins Irlish at Tobol and Irlish joins Ob near Belgor'ye and Ob finally discharges into the Arctic ocean. The river Ural discharges into the Caspian Sea (Figure 19).

It was in the 1970s that a scheme was proposed to divert the waters of the Irtysh river, which pours annually 28 billion cubic metres of water into the Ob, to southwards in two stages: (1) withdrawal of water from the lower Irtysh, the Tobol and the Ob much below the confluence with the Irtysh at

Figure 19

Central Asia: Proposed diversions of river water including projects transferring water from Siberia to Central Asia

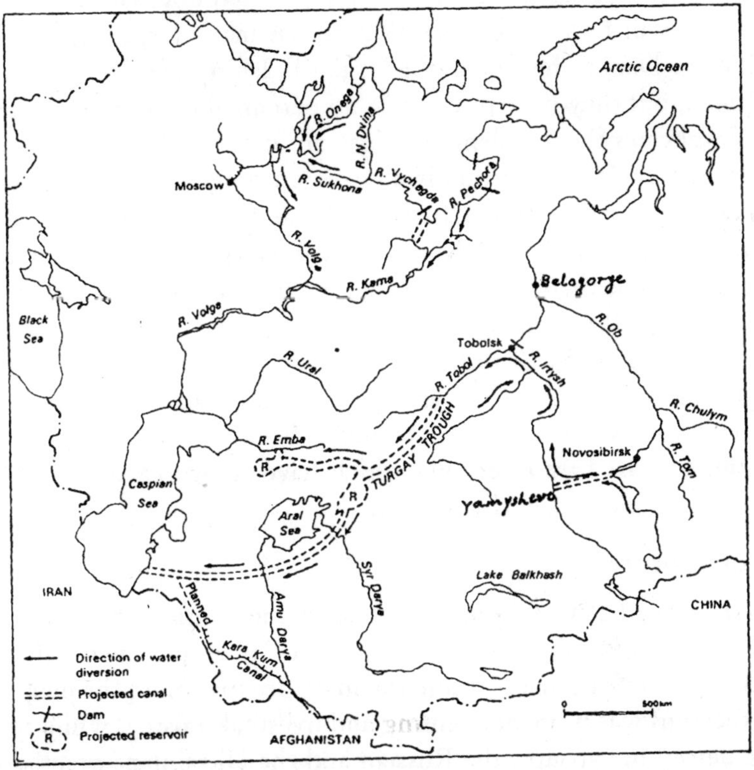

Source: M.I. Lvovichm Micklin (1977) and others.

Belogorge, and (2) withdrawal of water from the Chulym and Tom rivers as well as from the Novosibirsk reservoir on the Ob, with the transfer of water through a canal to a proposed reservoir at Yamyshevo on the Irtysh and onward by canal to Kurgan, and (3) a combination of the first two, with withdrawal of water from the Novosibirsk reservoir on the Ob river and transfer by canal to the Yamyshevo reservoir on the Irtysh as well as withdrawal from a proposed reservoir on the

Tabol.[8] The carrying of water in a north-south direction through the Turgay Trough towards the interfluve between the Syr Darya and Amu Darya would involve a canal of 2,000 to 2,500 km (Figure 19). However, the plan has not materialized.

It will be seen that Kazakhstan has many large rivers like the Syr Darya, the Irtysh, the Ural, Illi, Ishim, the Chu and the Emba, but they have practically no perennial tributaries which complicates the problem of irrigation. It can make good use of its vast reserve of groundwater. According to one estimate, there are large artesian basin of fresh water underlying the desert sands of Kyzyl Kum, Bet-pak-Dala, and Ust Yurt at depth of less than 80 metres (Figure 19). The source of water is the mountain regions of the south. The ice-melt water amounting to 5,000 million cubic metres annually percolates underground to join the artesian reservoirs and it is believed that this water can be obtained through boring without affecting the base reservoirs which have an aggregate of 4,000 billion cubic metres (Figure 19).

Agriculture

The agricultural economy has undergone considerable change since the independence of the state. In 1924 and even before that, as part of Soviet Union, the main occupation of the people (Kazakh) was nomadic herding and livestock raising, while the other ethnic groups, the Russian and the Ukrainians practised sedentary agriculture in the northern steppes, and the Uzbeks cultivated the land in the southern part of Kazakhstan.

Later on a change occurred, owing to land reform introduced by the Soviets, and nomadic herding was no longer the sole occupation of the Kazakhs. It was confined only to the herdsmen, and not to the entire community moving from pasture to pasture. Most of the Kazakhs took to sedentary agriculture. It was only in the summer that the herdsmen took to the higher mountain grazing grounds.

Table 29
Agriculture: Principal Crops

(in 000 metric tonnes)

	2000	*2001*	*2002*
Wheat	9073.5	12706.8	12670.0
Rice	214.3	198.7	199.1
Barley	1663.6	2243.8	2208.9
Maize	248.8	320.4	435.2
Ryen	48.3	43.4	106.5
Oats	181.8	220.3	183.2
Millet	62.3	65.3	39.2
Buckwheat	28.7	44.9	29.6
Other cereals	25.8	28.8	24.8
Potatoes	1632.6	2185	2268.8
Sugarbeet	272.7	282.5	372.2
Drypers	09.2	13.6	26.7
Sunflower seed	104.6	149.0	189.8
Safflower seed	25.4	25.0	27.9
Cabbages	262.7	303.5	321.8
Tomatoes	387.0	447.2	448.9
Cucumber	190.6	218.1	257.4
Onion	302.0	348.9	309.9
Carrots	163.6	189.1	214.5
Apples	144.6	132.4	110.5
Plums	7.4	6.7	12.7
Strawberries	5.3	5.7	12.5
Grapes	61.6	43.0	20.3
Watermelon	421.6	619.0	628.8
Other fruits	22.5	12.2	26.9
Tobacco leaves	16.2	15.0	15.8
Cotton lint	93.5	112.7	90.4
Pears	10.2	9.4	9.6
Cherries	12.0	6.4	14.0

Sources: Europa, 2004, Vol. II, p. 2419.

Kazakhstan agriculture can be best understood if it is divided into three regions and the characteristics of agriculture be analysed in respect of each region. These regions are: (1) the north-western, and the north-eastern region, (2) the centre and the south-western region, and (3) the south and the south-eastern region.

Northern Kazakhstan

Northern Kazakhstan, climatically, is a part of West Siberian lowlands. It consists of Chernozem soil, and in its southern part, it is a dry steppe with dark chestnut soil in the north. The average annual rainfall is about 40 cm and is drained by the Tobol and Ishim rivers which are the left hand tributaries of Irtish river. It is Kazakhstan's granery of wheat in the north, while in the southern part of this region dairy farming and sheep rearing are practised.

Fluctuation in climate leads to sharp fluctuations in yield. For example, in 1976 the production of wheat was over 16 million tonnes. In 1977 the production came down to 8.5 million tonnes. In 1980 it was 16.4 million tonnes and increased to 18.2 million tonnes in 1992, but in 1993 it came down to 11.5 and in 1994 to only 9 million tonnes. There was practically no shrinkage in area under wheat in 1992 as well as in 1993 and 1994. The area under wheat was 12 million hectares but the yield per hectare came down from 1,318 kg in 1981 to 909 kg in 1992 and 717 kg in 1993. This was mainly due to fluctuations in climates. The same situation is seen when the climate is favourable when production was 9 million tonnes in 2000 but rose to 12 million tonnes in 2001 and 2002 respectively. Lands which were in pastoral use were converted into state farms on a large scale for grain production between 1954 and 1960 and grain production is based on advanced mechanization.

Apart from wheat, oats and millet are also grown. The area under oats was 0.6 million hectares with a production of 0.8 million tonnes in 1994. The area under millet was 0.36 million hectares with a production 0.13 million tonnes in 1994. The northern most region is crossed by the Trans-Siberian Railway. There are meat packing plants and flour mills in this section.

Towards the drier south of the region the raising of sheep for meat and wool is dominant. Livestock is reared with the help of root crops. In the south of Kazakhstan there is a preponderance of saline areas which are not suitable for cultivation and consequently pastures dominate.

Western Kazakhstan consists of dry steppe. The river Ural touches its northern boundary and flows through the centre of the region. Agriculture is mainly developed in the north with sharp fluctuations in yield. The main crops are millet and mustard.

The north-eastern region is drained by the Irtysh river. In the north, it is rainfed agriculture and grows wheat and millet, while in the south of this region wheat is grown with the help of irrigation. Cattle and sheep are raised extensively. Sunflower is a dominant crop. The extreme north-eastern region is covered by the province of Pavlodar where the river Irtysh flows through the centre of the region from south to north. There also the main crops are wheat and millet.

Central Kazakhstan

It is drained by the upper Ishim in the northern section. It is a steppe region with black earth as well as brown soil. The northern section is hilly and upland while its south-western section is a rolling plain. The average precipitation in the central region is about 30 cm. Summers are hot and winters are very cold. Among the food-grains wheat, oats and millet are cultivated. The northern and eastern sections being hilly, dairy farming is the dominant occupation. In the western part agriculture is rainfed, while in the south-west sheep rearing is the main occupation. This section belongs to Akmolinsk province.

In the heart of central Kazakhstan lies the biggest province of Karaganda which covers about six per cent of the total area of Kazakhstan. The whole area consists of dry steppe in the form of upland and the southern portion includes parts of Bet Pak Dala desert. There are two streams in the area, Sary Su and Nura and they discharge into inland lakes. Grain farming is carried out in the northern part of the central region and the main crops are wheat and vegetables. The southern section is semi-desert and desert where cattle and sheep rearing is done for meat and wool.

In the south-west of the region, lies KzylOrda towards the east of Aral Sea (Figure 18). A major portion is covered by sandy desert (Kara Kum and Kzyl Kum). Agriculture is possible with the help of irrigation from Syr Darya which flows through the middle of the region and falls in the Aral Sea. The chief crop is rice. A big stone dam has been built on the Syr Darya at Tas Buget near Kzyl Orda (province) to provide irrigation to rice fields. In the desert, sheep and camel raising are important.

Southern Kazakhstan

Southern Kazakhstan may be considered in four parts: (a) south-western part of Kazakhstan, (b) a narrow strip of fertile irrigated land south of the Chu river, (c) the region lying to the east of lake Balkhash, and (d) strip along the Ili river centring on Almati (Alma Ata).

South-western part of Kazakhstan

It is the cotton region of Kazakhstan. It is drained by Syr Darya. The range Kara Tau lies in the east and the desert Kzyl Kum in the west. It is the main cotton producing region of Kazakhstan and Chimkent the capital of the province of southern Kazakhstan lies in the rich cotton and fruit growing area.

Region lying south of Chu river

This fertile irrigated strip of land lies south of Chu river which alongwith the river Talas provides irrigation for growing crops like sugarbeet, cotton, wheat, rice and tobacco. In the drier areas cattle, sheep, horses and camels are reared (Figure 18).

The Taldy Kurgan region lying south-east of Balkhash

Here, irrigated agriculture is common on the mountain slopes and the region produces wheat, sugarbeet, rice, opium tobacco and cotton. In the dry areas, cattle and sheep are raised. At the extreme eastern end of lake Bulkhash lies the town of Burlyu-Tobe which is the centre of fisheries (Figure 18).

Strip centring on Almati (Alma Ata)

This region is 130 km wide along the Ili river from the western end of lake Balkhash to the Chinese border. It is hilly in the south with sandy desert in the north-west. The chief crops cultivated with the help of irrigation on the southern mountain slopes are wheat, sugarbeet, tobacco, opium, garden fruits like apple and grapes.

It should thus be noted that agricultural economy in Kazakhstan has undergone transformation from primarily cattle breeding to production of grains, cotton and other crops like tobacco, andmustard. In brief, it can be said that the northern sectors with their rich black earth grows cereals. In the south cotton grows well on lands near the rivers. Kazakhstan has rich orchards and vineyards which account for 95,000 hectares of cultivated land. Kazakhstan is also noted for its livestock, particularly its sheep from which excellent quality wool is obtained. In 2002, there were 4.2 million cattle, 10.5 million sheep and goats. In 2002, the total cereal production was 15.84 million tonnes. There is great fluctuation in the production of cereal from year to year.

Kazakhstan's Problems of Agriculture

With a total population of about 16 million and growth rate of 1.1 per cent per annum, the production of food grains needs to be increased. Production can be increased by two methods: (1) by bringing more lands under cultivation, and (2) by increasing the yield per hectare. As regards bringing more lands under the plough, one is reminded of the great land reclamation of 1954-62 when Kazakhstan was a part of Soviet Union. About 23 million hectares of virgin and fallow land were brought under the plough and cultivated with spring wheat. About 550 state grain farms were set up, and gradually more steppe and semi-arid pasture lands were brought under cultivation and it is estimated that between 1954 and 1970, production increased four-folds. Apparently there was great success in food grain production, but it was at the cost of soil deterioration. If the area is semi-arid or arid and rainfall is between 10 and 20 cms, crops like wheat can be produced with the help of irrigation, drawing water from surface flow and underground water, but the cultivation will not be eco-friendly and adverse climatic conditions will lead to land deterioration.

Wheat monoculture in the areas of 'virgin lands scheme' gradually converted the area into a 'dust bowl' as experienced in the USA, in the 1930s. During the wheat growing season, strong and desiccating westerly and south-westerly winds usually blow into Tselinograd oblast and Tselinograd city, the centre of the virgin lands scheme, and the area experienced dust storm on 53 days per year on an average.[9] Thus, it looked desirable to make changes in the cropping pattern and crops which are suited to dry farming conditions and require much less quantity of water, like barley, millet, (small and big), oats, rye, maize, peas and pulses be included in the cropping pattern on a large scale. In 2002, its total production of cereals was about 16 million tonnes; the production of wheat was 12.6 million tonnes. In 1993, the dryland crops production was 11 million tonnes, and that of wheat 12.6 million tonnes. In 2002, total production of cereals was about 16 million tonnes; dryland crops were only 4 million tonnes. Seeing the fluctuations in the production of wheat, there is a need to reorient the cropping pattern. Dry farming techniques should be perfected and machinery better suited to Kazakhstan's soil and climatic conditions be introduced.

In case of southern Kazakhstan, there are the desert margins where the drought resistant crops are grown: like cotton, mustard and linseed. It is necessary that improved varieties be introduced so that their yield per hectare may increase. The loess covered uplands and mountain slopes of Kurgan and Almati (Alma Ata) have extensive orchards and produce good vegetable crops. The orchards include apples, grapes, melons, pears, peaches and plums. Food processing and canning industries should be developed and export trade be built up. Table 29 shows the variety of fruits and vegetables grown in Kazakhstan in different years.

Kazakhstan can enter world market by exporting quality fruits and vegetables at competitive prices to south, south-east and west Asia.

One of the major occupations of the people of Kazakhstan is raising of cattle, sheep and goats, horses and camels. Table 29 shows the position of livestock from 2000 to 2002.

Kazakhstan is famous for its meat packing industry as it has a large number of cattle and about 10.4 million sheep and goats. The dry lands of the desert margins, as well as the mountains, in early summer months and in the spring, provide good opportunity for grazing. In the winter months, the cattle, the sheep and goats are brought down to the desert margin while in spring they return to the mountains. In summers Kazakhstan grows ample quantities of lucerne which provides good feed in winter months.

Kazakhstan sheep are famous for their wool and sheep skin. The sheep have very fine fleece and the breed is known as 'Akharomerino', which is a new cross-breed derived from the Australian merino and the native sheep. Akharomerino is well adapted to the environment of Kazakhstan. Kazakhstan wool production in 2002 was 24,000 tonnes (greasy) and 14,000 tonnes clean wool. It also produces sufficient number of Karakul sheep skin. These skins are taken from new born lambs and are very popular in the world fur market.

Table 30
Livestock

(in 000 heads)

	2000	*2001*	*2002*
Horses	970	976	989
Cattle	3998	4107	4282
Buffaloes	96	991	98
Camels	964	1076	1124
Sheep	8725	8939	9208
Goats	931	1042	1271
Chickens	18623	19705	21279

Table 31
Livestock Products

(in 000 metric tonnes)

	2000	*2001*	*2002*
Beef and veel	306.3	287.0	297.0
Mutton and lamb	91.2	91.7	93.9
Goat meat	3.9	5.0	7.2
Poultry meat	33.3	33.8	36.1
Cow's milk	3730.0	3922.0	4068.0
Sheep milk	34.8	35.0	40.7
Goat milk	9.7	10.5	11.0
Cheese	10.8	10.2	11.2
Butter	4.4	3.9	4.0
Hen egg	93.8	1003.0	116.6
Wool greasy	22.9	23.6	23.8
Wool clean	13.7	14.2	14.3
Cattle hide	34.8	34.5	36.1
Sheep skin	9.9	10.3	10.4

Source: Europa, 2004, Vol. II, p. 2119.

Kazakhstan meat industry is developed on most modern lines. The meat is processed in refrigeration and exported to other countries including the CIS, and Semipalatinsk has a huge meat factory resembling the Chicago type, meat packing plant.

It can organize its poultry on lines similar to that of Denmark and export eggs to Middle East countries.

The annual production of fresh water fish is about 31,000 tonnes (2004). This production can easily be doubled or trebled to achieve a flourishing fish industry.

Minerals Resources

Kazakhstan is a storehouse of non-ferrous metals: copper, lead, zinc, silver, chrome, nickel and molybdenum, antimony, tin, bauxite, gold, tungsten, cobalt, titanium, manganese and corundum (Table 32).

The reserves of copper are estimated at 10 million tonnes. Copper deposits occur at various places in Kazakhstan. There are three large deposits in the upland of Central Kazakhstan: (a) in the southwest of Karaganda province at Dzhezkazgan, (b) on the lake Balkhash at Kounradskiy in the northern part of the lake, and (c) Maykain and Boshcekul in the Pavlodar province. Copper smelting and refining takes place at Uspenskiy on the Balkhash, for the Kounradskiy mine. At Karsakpay there is an old smelting plant and at Bolshoy-Dzhezkazgan there are modern refining plants. Copper is also mined at Gulbokoye in east Kazakhstan while zinc is mined at Dzungarian Gates, Ala Tau and Kara Tau. Lead and zinc are also mined at Leninogorsk, at Kara Tau range and at Kantagi in south Kazakhstan provinces. Precious metal like chrome and nickel are mined in the northern Muyorlzhars mountain just south of Orsk Khalilovo near Batamshinskiy (formerly Kimpersayskiy). The production of refined copper in 2002 was 0.43 million tonnes. Chorme resources are also available at Donskoy and Khrom Tau in northern Mugodzar mountain. There are good deposits of manganese, mined in Ulu Tau range at Dzhezdinskiy and in the Mangyshlak peninsula in the

Table 32
Mineral Resources

	2000	*2001*	*2002*
Iron ore	13.82 million tonnes	29.6 million tonnes	33.5 million tonnes
Copper ore	0.43 million tonnes	34.8 million tonnes	36.6
Nickel ore	3.0 million tonnes	-	-
Bauxite	3.7 million tonnes	-	-
Lead ore	.04 million tonnes	Lead and zinc combined – 5.7 million tonnes	6.2 million tonnes
Zinc	.32 million tonnes	-	-
Manganese ore	.72 million tonnes	-	-
Chromite	2.6 million tonnes	-	-
Titanium	8.2 million tonnes	-	-
Silver ore	0.92 million tonnes	-	-
Uranium	1.7 million tonnes	-	-
Gold (kg)	28171	-	-
Asbestos	0.23	-	-

north-east of Caspian. Tin and tungsten are mined in Kalba Range at Ubaredmet. Again tungsten and molybdenum are mined at Akchatau north of Balkhash in the Karganda province, while corundum is mined at Turgay in Kustanai province. Kazakhstan has widely scattered gold deposits. It is found in Akmolinsk enclave of the Stepnyak area in the Akmolinsk province, and also at Zharma Akzhal and at Zhangis, in Semipalatinek province at Tobe, at Maykain in Pavlodar province. Gold is mined in the province of East Kazakhstan at various places, e.g., Samarsokoya, Kuludzhunskly and at Palattsy.

Gold is also mined in the Altay mountain. The principal centres are: Leninogorsk, Zyryanovsk and Belousovka. The production of gold in 2002 was 28,170 kg. East Kazakhstan provides many other minerals like silver ores.

Iron ore is mined in the south-west and south-east of Karaganda and its production in 2002 was 13.8 million metric tonnes.

Power Resources

Coal deposits occur at Ekibastuz in Pavlodar province but the most important area of coal production is Karanganda coal basin. Deposits of coal occur in the Mugodzhar mountain and at Lenger and in Ulu Tau at Baykonur, also at Berchogur and Kurashasayskiy. Coal is also mined at Kara Tau ranges of the Mangyshlak peninsula. In the Akmolinsk province coal is mined at Petropavlovsk along the upper Kenderlyk river in the Saur range on the Russia-China border in East Kazakhstan province. Coal mines occur at Keltemashat and at Chopak. The total coal production in 2000 was 74.8 million tonnes but in 2002 the production was 70.6 million tonnes.

Hydroelectricity is produced at Ul'ba on the Ul'ba river near Leninogorsk; at Ablaketka just south of U'st Kamonogorsk on the Irtysh river; and at Glubokoye in east Kazakhstan.

High grade crude oil is obtained from Dossor and Makat; Baychunas, Iskininskiy, Kulsary and Koschagyl on the lower Emba river. There are natural gas fields in the Guryev province in the Caspian region below sea level.

Proven oil reserves in 1996 were 2,000 million tonnes and according to another estimate the total reserve (on shore and off shore) of petroleum are 4,500 million metric tonnes and those of natural gas 5,900,000 m cubic metres.

The Karachaganak field has reserve of 20,000,000 million cu ft (20 trillion cu ft) or 566,320 million cu metres[2]. The production of oil in 2002 was 42 million tonnes and that of natural gas 13137 million cubic metres (Table 33).

Table 33

Power Resources

(in 000 metric tonnes)

	2000	*2001*	*2002*
Coal	74.8 million tonnes	76.4 million tonnes	70.6 million tonnes
Crude petroleum	30.6 million tonnes	30.0 million tonnes	42.0 million tonnes
Natural gas	11542 million (cu metre)	11610 million (cu metre)	13137 million (cu metre)
Electric energy in million KWh	51635	55384	58478

Industry

Kazakhstan was industrialized in the Soviet period with non-ferrous metallurgy, heavy engineering and chemical industries. In 2002, the production of steel was 4.8 million tonnes, pig iron 4.68 million tonnes, chemical fibre 1,900 tonnes, paper 2,100 tonnes, cement 2.12 million tonnes, fabrics 14 million sq metres (2002), copper refined 0.45 million tonnes (Table 34).

Table 34

Industry

(in 000 metric tonnes)

	2000	*2001*	*2002*
Wheat flour	1.7 million	-	-
Raw sugar	0.28 million tonnes	0.34	0.39
Cigarette (million)	19292	-	-
Woven cotton fabrics (million sq metre)	5.0	8.0	14
Cotton yarn	.001 (million)	-	-
Sulphuric acid	.63 million metric tonnes	-	-
Motor spirit	1.9	1.5	1.7
Kerosene	.063	-	-
Cement	1.1 million tonnes	2.0	2.1
Pig-iron	4.0 million tonnes	3.9	4
Crude steel	4.7 million tonnes	4.6	4.8

It should be noted that non-ferrous metallurgy is one of the leading branches of industry in Kazakhstan. Lead, copper and zinc smelting are the most important branches of industry. The following four regions are outstanding in respect of non-ferrous metal industry.

1. *Eastern Kazakhstan:* There are polymetallic and copper industries (the Ust-Kamennogorsk lead-zinc combine, the Leninogorsk and Irtysh polymetallic combine, the Zyryanovsk lead combine).

2. *Karaganda Region:* Known for copper industry (the Balkhash-karsak-pay and Dzhezhazgan copper smelting plants with Kounradskly and Uspenskly mines).

3. *Southern Kazakhstan:* The polymetallic industry (Chimkent lead plant, the Achisay polymetallic combined).

4. *Taldy-Kuragan Region:* Polymetallic industry, Tekeli lead zinc combine.

So far as the ferrous metal industry is concerned it is found in Aktyubinsk. The iron ore reserves and chromite reserves are substantial.

The industrial products include cotton yarn, fabrics, footwear, sulphuric acid, synthetic rubber, rubber tyres, building bricks, pig-iron, crude steel. Table 34 shows production in different years.

Some parts of Kazakhstan are highly industrialized and the most important sectors are associated with the transformation of raw material, including metal processing, chemicals, machine buildings, textile and food processing.

Kazakhstan's aluminum industry resources are located in Arkadak. Bauxite is sent by rail to Kamennogorsk where it is converted into aluminum sheets. It is interesting to note that the integrated iron and steel plant opened in Kazakhstan as early as 1960 and began to sustain the small steel works at Temir Tau and Aktyubinsk. The Karaganda metallurgical plant situated at Temir-Tau where Samarkand reservoir provides processed water to many blast furnaces.

Engineering industries in Kazakhstan are located at Pavlodar, Karaganda and Chimkent and specialized in the manufacture of coal mining machinery, metallurgical plant and equipment. Guryev makes oil industry equipment. Pavlodar has a large tractor workshop and Almaty manufactures agricultural implements.

Kazakhstan manufactures phosphatic fertilizer. There is a super phosphate plant at Dzhambul in the south and it makes use of phosphate obtained locally at Kara-Tau. The production ranges between four and five million tonnes and the major production comes from Aktyubinsk super-phosphate plants.

Other Industries

Industries based on agricultural and livestock products are well distributed in Kazakhstan. Meat packing plants are among the largest in the country. They are located at Ural'sk, Petropavlovsk and Semipalatinsk. Beet sugar refineries are located at Almaty (Alma Ata), Merke, Taldy-Kurgan, Karabulak, and Dzhambul. Fruit preserving factories are in Chimket, Dzhambul, and at Almaty (Alma Ata). Industries related to flour milling, tanning, leather products, wool washing, cotton ginning and cotton seed oil extraction are well established.

Transport and Means of Communication

The development of transport is a recent phenomenon in Kazakhstan. Transport development took place with the agricultural and industrial development of the state. During the last seven decades, there has been a sharp change in the agricultural economy of Kazakhstan. Prior to that the population was primarily engaged in nomadic herding. Till 1972, Trans-Caspian Railway from Chkalov to Tashkant served the whole of this vast area.

With the development of railway, Kazakhstan's economy was entirely transformed and through the railways, it became possible to develop the resources of even the remotest areas.

Figure 20

Central Asia: Mineral Resources

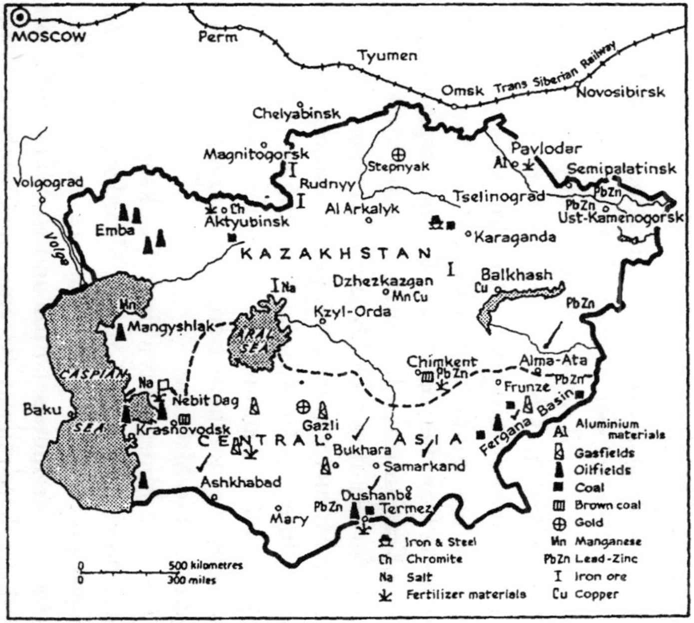

Source: Mathieson, R.S. (1975), *The Soviet Union – An Economic Geography*, Norwitch, p. 251.

Even the population of small settlements were joined by the railways, and the settlement of Syr-Dar'inkiy in the Kyzyl Kum desert was raised to the status of a town.

The earliest pattern of the railway line in Kazakhstan was from north to south owing to the absence of Navigable rivers in the state but later on, apart from north-south railway line, east-west line parallel to the Trans-Siberian railway was built.

Kazakhstan railway system can be divided into four groups (Figure 20).

1. The Turkoib Railway: construction virtually started in 1927, between Semi-palatinsk which was a terminus of branch of Trans-Siberian railway leading from Novosibirsk to Chimket and Arys, on the Trans-Caspian line. In the south it goes upto Almaty (Alma Ata) where a branch line connects it at Berlik with the central railway coming from Petropovlovsk (Trans-Caspian line).
2. The Trans-Kazakh line from Petropavlovsk to Karaganda and further down to Dzhambul, Lenger and Chimkent. From Mointy a branch line goes to Kounradskiy while the main line runs to Chu and continues to Dzhambul and goes west to a point Aral'sk on the Aral sea, and finally crosses the northern border of Kazakhstan near Ural'sk and runs to Moscow.
3. The Orenburg-Aktyubinsk-Tashkent and the newly extended Astrakhan-Guryev, Chardzou (Figure 21).
4. Dushanbe: It takes coal from Karaganda, other non-ferrous metals, cotton and wool (Trans-Caspian line).

Of the three railway systems, the Orenburg Tashkent line is the oldest. It was constructed in the year 1906. Before the completion of this line, Kazakhstan cotton trade was not in a flourishing state, so was the case with Uzbekistan, and much of the cotton textiles that were produced in the two regions obtained raw cotton from Egypt and India. So, in 1906, a railway line from Taskent towards north to Orenburg was completed. With this facility, cotton could be transported north-west and grain and lumber (from Siberia) southwards. In

Figure 21

Central Asia: The Development of the Transportation System

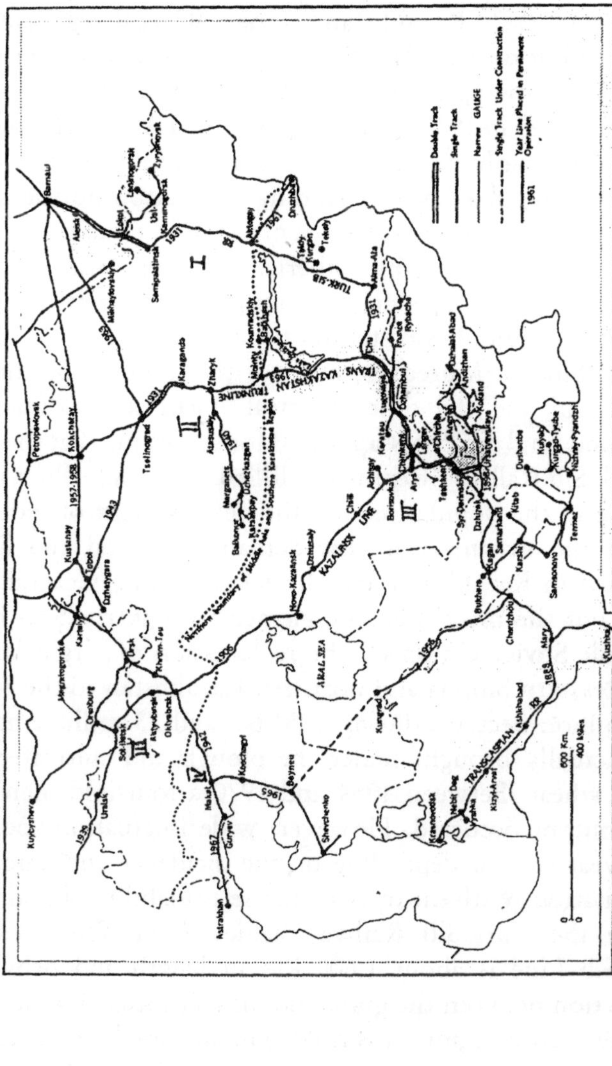

Source: Lydolph Paul E., (1970), *Geography of the USSR*, New York, p. 265.

about a decade and a half, after the construction of this Kazalinsk line (as it came to be known) was much over-burdened and need was felt for the construction of Turk-Sib Railway, (Turkistan-Siberian) from Semipalatinsk to Arys on the Kazakhstan Line (Oremburg-Tashkent). Construction on the Turk-Sib Line started in 1912, but work was stopped owing to World War I and again started in 1927 and completed in 1931. This railway joined Almaty (Alma Ata) of Lake Balkhash, reached Chimkent and joined Arys. It was built with the objectives of sending raw cotton northeastward into the developing industrial centres of Siberia, and to bring lumber and grain from Siberia. At this time in 1931, Kazakhstan was producing enough food grains for its population and only one-tenth of the requirement was met by western Siberia. Moreover, most of the lumber consumed in Kazakhstan and the other Central Asian states came from Volga and Ural region. It appeared for sometime that the hopes of Turk-Sib Railway were not fulfilled. But gradually with the increase in the population and the development of industrialization and urbanization, the demand for food and lumber increased in Kazakhstan and the neighbouring Central Asian states, but the most dramatic element was introduced by the erstwhile Soviet Union by the reclamation of virgin lands in south-western Siberia and northern Kazakhstan to the tune of 30.9 million hectares during 1954-62, and 23 million hectares were actually brought under the plough and cultivated with spring wheat. Between 1954 and 1970 a four-fold increase in grain output occurred. However, wide fluctuations occurred from year to year depending on the incidence and amount of precipitation. With the increase in the availability of grain from Siberia the Turk-Sib Railway achieved its objectives. The Turk-Sib Line is about 1,600 km in length and provided a connection between the grain and lumber areas of west Siberia and the cotton region of Kazakhstan and the huge increase in the quantum of wheat production boosted trade between the former USSR and the Sinkiang province of China.

In 1953, the Trans-Kazakhstan trunk line was completed from Petropavlovsk towards south through Akmolinsk, Karaganda and Mointy to Balkhash and the main line ran from Moity to further south to Chu and runs west, parallel to Syr Darya and skirting the northern boundary, goes to Moscow.

Then there are the branch lines like Gur'yev-Kandaghach line which provides exit from the Emba oilfield. The line has been extended from Kandagach to Orsk in the north and goes beyond Kazakhstan to Sverdlovsk. This has opened up the rich nickel and chrome deposits of the north.

Kazakhstan has built a number of parallel branch lines which join major cities directly or provides access to the new mining and industrial areas (Figure 21).

Population

Kazakhstan has a total area of 2,717,300 sq km and a population of 15,403,000 (2004)[13] which gives a density per sq km in 2004 of 5.6; the female population of 8.49 million exceeds the male population of 7.97 million by a little more then 6 per cent.

The principal ethnic groups 1994 are shown in Table 6. Among the ethnic groups, the Kazakhs predominate and together with the Russians, they make up about 80 per cent of the total population of Kazakhstan.

There are nineteen provinces in Kazakhstan. The highest density of population is in the province of Almaty (Alma Ata) (20.5), Alma Ata was formerly the capital of Kazakhstan, but in 1995 the capital was shifted to Almola.

Next in importance are southern Kazakh province (16.1), followed by northern Kazakhstan province with a density of 13.7 persons per sq km, next is Karaganada province with a density of 11.3 and is followed by East Kazakhstan (9.7). Next in importance are Akmola (9.6) and Kustanai province (9.4). The lowest density is found in Dzhezkazgan (1.6).

Growth Rate

It will thus be seen that the population over the years shows a slow decline in the growth rate of population. The growth rate according ESCAP Population Data Sheet 2004 was 0.3 per cent per annum.

Around 22 per cent of the population is engaged in agriculture, hunting, forestry and fishing. About 27 per cent of the population is engaged in community, social and personal services; 22 per cent in trade (hotels). Thus, about three-fourths of the total employed persons are engaged in three professions and one-fourth in the rest of the professions.

There is great imbalance in the occupations. The number of people engaged in mining and industry is too small. If Kazakhstan is a storehouse of minerals, the people engaged in mining should be far greater than what they are today (2004).

Towns

Astana (formerly Akmola) is the capital of Kazakhstan. It is one of the most beautiful cities of Central Asia with a population of 313,000. The Almaty (Alma Ata) city was founded in 1854 as the Russian fort and was called Vernyy in 1885. Its name was changed to Alma Ata in 1921 and became the capital of Kazakhstan from 1929-95. It is situated in the picturesque foothills of the Trans–Ili Ala Tau and has a magnificent backdrop of mountain scenery. The rushing torrents from the mountain in the south and the existence of Lake Balkhash in the north add grace to its surroundings. The whole area between the city and the mountain is occupied by apple orchards. Almaty (Alma Ata) means "father of apples".

The city is divided into straight avenues which rise steeply. A branch line of about 12 km of Turk-Sib Railway climbs the foothills and runs into the city. On either side of the long, straight asphalted street, there are two rows of tall poplars. The city contains a large number of splendid public buildings. The buildings are specially designed to withstand earthquakes;

tremors which frequently occur, and the location is rather unstable. This might be the reason for the authorities to change the site of the capital to Akmola and now it is Astana.

Almaty (Alma Ata) (1,129,400) is also an important industrial centre. It has a heavy machine-building industrial industry, spinning mills, fruit preserving and meat packing plants, tobacco factories, tanneries and saw mills. It is also a cultural centre. It has a university (established in 1928), a large library, Kazakh and Russian opera house, theatre and museums and is the seat of Kazakh Academy of Sciences. In 1997, the capital was shifted from Almaty to Akmola (formerly Isfelinograd) now known as Astana.

Karaganda

It is principally a coal mining centre. Its population in 2004 is estimated at about 800,000. It is situated in Central Kazakhstan to the north of Lake Balkhash. The city is known for its large iron and steel plant. The city was founded in 1926 and since then it has been rapidly progressing. The steel plant is located in the suburban city of Temir Tau or the iron mountain to the north-west of Karanganda. It receives its coal from the local mines as it is in the centre of the Karanganda coal basin and iron ore comes from Kustany province and its water supply is from the Nura river. Nura dries up in the summer. The town is located on a branch railway which connects it with the Trans-Siberian Railway which runs to the north. Coal also comes from Kuznetsk basin. Thus, Karaganda today is not only a mining town, but a town of many growing industries including iron and steel. The Karaganda coal fields has twenty working seams ranging in thickness from 1 to 8.5 metres and lie nearly in horizontal positions at depth between 50 and 300 metres. Most of the coal is produced by shift mines. The coal contains about 22 per cent ash and hence its use is limited to steel industry. The water supply comes from the reservoir built on the river Nura by erecting a dam. In the south-west of Karaganda, there are seven big copper refineries and

Karanganda is connected by railway to these refineries. Similarly there is a railway which connects Karaganda with the town of Balkhash.

Chimkent (Shymkent)

Along the base of Tein Shan, south-west of Dzhambul and west of Lenger lies Chimkent with a population estimated about 360,100. There are two other towns at a distance of 300 km from one another on the northwestern corner of Tien Shan engaged in chemical industry. Shymkent is said to be one of the largest smelting centres in Asia. Shymkent lies in a rich cotton and fruit growing area. Apart from lead works, it has a chemical plant for pharmaceutical products, cotton gins, flour mills and fruit processing machines.

Pavlodar

It is the capital of province Pavlodar with a population of 349,000 (1993). It is situated at the junction of the Irtysh river and the south Siberian railway. The left bank of the river is higher and drier and possesses rich mineral deposits. There are large copper deposits at Maykain about 60 km south-west of Pavlodar and gold mining is carried out at the site of Mayakain. Pavlodar has meat and tanning industries, flour mills and saw mills. There are salt brine lakes east of the Irtysh river near Pavlodar and chemicals are produced on the basis of salt extracted.

Semipalatinsk

Semipalatinsk is the capital of province of Semipalatinsk with a population of 342,000. It is situated at the junction of the Irtysh river and the Turksib railway. About 80 km south of Semipalatinsk lies Zhangis-Tobe and further 40 km south lies Zharma. Both are important gold mining centres. Semipalatinsk has a very big meat packing plant, tanning and textile industries and wool processing and lumber mills.

Ust'Kamemogorsk

It lies on the Irtysh river and has a zinc smelting plant. It also possesses tanning and vegetable oil industries. It falls in East Kazakhstan and has a population of 334,000. The hydroelectric station which provides electricity to Ust'Kamengogork lies at a distance of 16 km in the south at Irtysh river.

Aktyubinsk

It is the capital of province Aktyuibinsk with a population of 264,000. It is situated on the Orenburg-Tashkent Railway. It is situated in a brown soil steppe region surrounded by desert in the south. The rainfall varies between 25 and 40 cm the region is mainly devoted to livestock raising. There are extensive phosphate deposits south of Aktyubinsk. Aktyubinsk has electro-chemical and fertilizer manufacturing works.

Petropavlovsk

It is the capital of north Kazakhstan province which is the northern most province of Kazakhstan and is a part of the west Sibarian lowland. Its population in 2004 was 23,500. Petropavlovsk derives its support from the rich agricultural economy of the province which produces wheat, oats, millet, and dairy products.

Petropavlovsk, since long, has been a caravan trading centre and it is situated at the junction of the Trans-Siberian and the Trans-Kazakhstan railway. It has large packing plants, flour mills and tanneries and also manufactures agricultural machinery.

Kustanai

It is the capital of the Kustanai province in the extreme north-west of Kazakhstan and connects west Siberian lowland in the north and the Kazakhstan upland in the south. Kustanai is situated on the Tobol river and is an important station on the south-Siberian railway which divides the province in two parts:

the northern part producing wheat oats and millet, while the southern part is devoted mainly to cattle raising and specializes in dairy products and wool. The population in 2004 was 221,000.

Ural'sk

It is the capital of the north-west Kazakhstan province, and had a population of 195,000 in 2004. the town lies in the extreme north-west of the province on the river Ural which takes a turn at this point and flows to the south and drains in the Caspian Sea, and is crossed by Kazalinsk line (the railway coming from Aktyaubinsk proceeds further west from Ural'sk to Moscow). Thus, its location is at the junction of Ural river and the railway from Tashkent to Moscow. As the entire provinces is steppe land, the north cultivates crops (millet and wheat and mustard) while the south specializes in livestock. There are natural gas wells which are not yet exploited. The population in the north consists of Russians and in the south of Kazakhs. Ural'sk is a meat packing centre and processes wool and hides.

Temir Tau

It literally means iron mountain and is situated on a small seasonal river Nura and on the railway line running from Turkistan to Kustanay. It is very close to Karaganda coal basin. The establishment of a hydroelectric plant and the erection in 1994 of the first steel mill producing about 2 million tonnes of steel gave a boost to this town. Its population in 1993 was 213,000.

Kzyl-Orda

It means red capital. For sometimes it was the capital of Kazakhstan when in 1929, the capital was shifted to Alma Ata. At present it is the capital of the Kzyl Orda province and had population of 164,000. It is one of the most arid provinces of Kazakhstan. The Syr Darya flows through it and the eastern and northern coast of Aral Sea falls within its borders. A stone dam has been built on Syr Darya near Kzyl Orda at Tas Buget and provides irrigation for rice cultivation. It is located on the railway that runs from Chimkent to Moscow and also has the advantage of location on the Syr Darya river. There are extensive deposits of phosphorite and salt peter and sodium and magnesium sulphate along Aral seashore. Chief industries are rice polishing, meat packing and food canning.

Kokchetav

It is the capital of Kokchetav province and is situated on the central Kazakh railway which runs from Balkhash to Petropavlosk. The whole region is a wooded steppe zone and as the rainfall is adequate and soil is black, the economy of the region is based on agriculture and wheat, oat and millet are the principal crops along with dairying. Kokchelav is an important health centre. Meat packing, floor milling and tanning are important industries. It has a population of 144,000.

Ekibastuz

The town is located in the Pavolodar province and lies on the railway running from China and entering Kazakhstan from the east. Ekibastuz is situated at a distance of 50 km from Pavlodar, and has extensive coal deposits. In 2004, its population was 127,200.

Taldy Kurgan

It is the capital of Taldy Kurgan province and had a population of 125,000. It is a small province established in 1994 and contains almost half the area of Lake Balkhash. It is situated in the midst of sugar beet region and sugar mills, flour mills and rice polishing mills are located here.

On the mountain slopes, wheat, rice and large quantities of sugar beet are produced. Cotton is also grown and in the drier areas sheep and cattle are raised. The Turk-Sib Railway passes through the middle of the province. There are lead and zinc mines and it takes full advantage of Lake Balkhash and fisheries are developed at eastern end of the lake at Burlyu-Robe. Taldy Kurgan is known for sugar, flour milling and rice polishing.

Trade

Trading Partners

Exports

There are seventeen countries to which Kazakhstan exports its commodities. It exported goods worth about 800 million dollars to various countries like China and some European countries, Central Asian countries, Russia, Ukraine and Korea. Of the total exports of about 800 million dollars one-fourth went to Burmuda, about one fifth to Russia, one-fourth to two countries of Europe: Netherland and Italy. Seventy per cent of the exports went to four countries of the world and the remaining exports to thirteen countries of the world (Table 35).

Table 35

Trading Partners: Exports

(in US Million Dollars)

Countries	*2000*	*2001*	*2002*	*Percentage to total export 2002*
Bermuda	1358.1	1221.2	2011.2	25.3
China	670.3	655.5	1020.2	12.8
Finland	-	56.1	48.6	0.60
Germany	566.6	509.7	218.6	2.76
Italy	891.9	970.9	921.6	11.6
Korea	-	45.4	49.3	0.61
Kyrgyzstan	58.5	87.1	107.6	1.35
Netherlands	240.0	145	123.2	15.5
Poland	71.2	164.2	320.4	4.0
Russia	1783.9	1748.4	1524.2	19.2
Switzerland	497.6	407.3	786.8	9.96
Tajikistan	-	61.3	46	0.59
Turkey	-	74.4	98	1.25
Ukraine	268.5	490.5	291.8	3.6
UK	231	295	132	1.2
USA	211	159.1	118.8	1.4
Uzbekistan	139.2	148.2	103.6	1.31

Imports

The imports of Kazakhstan in 2002 were much less than its exports – about half the imports came from Russia and one-fifth from Germany and USA. Thus, 70 per cent of the imports came from Russia, Germany and USA and the remaining imports of 30 per cent came from other fourteen countries (Table 36).

Table 36

Trading Partners: Imports

(in US Million Dollars)

Countries	*2000*	*2001*	*2002*	*Percentage to total import 2002*
Belarus	39.9	46.1	54.4	0.99
China	154	169.2	304.8	5.5
Finland	57.4	69.1	68.3	1.2
France	75.4	138.4	107.5	1.9
Germany	333.7	471.4	565.3	10.3
Italy	155	266	212.6	3.2
Japan	105.5	140.2	161.6	2.9
Korea	82.5	106.5	107.2	1.9
Netherlands	64.7	82.4	85.6	1.5
Poland	58.8	59.3	72.2	1.3
Russia	2459.8	2890.9	2540.4	46.5
Switzerland	54.3	65.8	57.1	1.0
Turkey	142.6	131.2	166.8	3.0
Ukraine	79.8	154.9	215.6	3.9
UK	219.4	246.3	255.7	4.6
USA	276.9	341.6	637.7	11.6
Uzbekistan	73.2	80.2	84.9	1.5

Pattern of Trade in Kazakhstan

Export

The total value of the exports from Kazakhstan in 2002 was 9287.7 million US$. Of this, mineral products consisted of 5951 million US$ (60 per cent) and the base metal were exported in

2002 of the value of 2237.9 million US$ (23 per cent). The remaining 17 per cent consisted of vegetables products, chemical products along with pearls and semi-precious stones (Table 37).

Table 37

Value of Exports

(in US million dollars)

Exports	*2000*	*2001*	*2002*
Vegetable Products	559.7	392.7	412.5
Mineral Products	4790.6	5028.8	5951.2
Chemical Products	378.2	405.9	418.9
Pearls, precious and semi-precious stones	387.6	254.6	267.2
Base metal	2279.7	2109.9	2237.9

Imports

In respect of imports, the total value of imports was 5994.6 million US$. Of the total imports, machinery, mechanical appliances and electrical equipments were of the value of 1846.4 million US $ 33.6. The minerals products were of the value of 826 million US$. Chemical products and transport equipment were of the value of 1,528 million US$ (28 per cent). Transportation equipment were of the value of 793.3 million US$ (14 per cent) (Table 38).

Table 38

Value of Imports

(in US million dollars)

	2000	*2001*	*2002*
Prepared food stuff	289.9	331.0	3209.9
Mineral products	657.6	904.4	826.3
Chemical products	545.8	667.1	706.1
Plastic and rubber	193.2	293.8	265.9
Base metal	562.9	889.5	735.5
Machinery, mechanical appliances and electrical equipment	1402.2	1852.6	1846.6
Transport equipment	563.0	625.0	793.0

Notes

1. U.N. ESCAP Population Data Sheet 2004.
2. *The Europa World Year Book (1998)*, Vol. II, p. 1933.
3. Lydolph, Paul E. (1964), *Geography of the USSR*, New York, p. 234.
4. Shabad, Theodore (1961), *Geography of the USSR*, New York, p. 341.
5. National Commission on Agriculture, Vol. V, New Delhi, 1976, p. 80.
6. Symons, Leslie, et al., *The Soviet Union, A Systematic Geography*, London, 1983.
7. Ibid., pp. 84-85.
8. Symons Leslie, (1983), *The Soviet Union*, London, p. 84
9. Mathrison, R.S., *The Soviet Union*, London, p. 252.
10. *Europa World Year Book (1998)*, Vol. II, p. 2420.
11. *Statesman Year Book*, p. 784.
12. *Europa World Year Book* (2004), Vol. II, p. 2420.
13. ESCAP Population Data Sheet, U.N. Building, Bangkok, 2004.

8

Central Asia: Historical Significance

The Central Asian states are landlocked and surrounded by powerful countries. In the east lies China, further east is Mongolia, in the north lies Russia and in the north-west is Turkey. Towards the south lies Afghanistan and Iran. Like Belgium, which has been the cockpit of Europe, Central Asia, because of its bridge between Asia and Europe, has in the past been subject to subjugation by various nations.

The historical significance of Central Asia may be considered from 3000 BC to 2000 BC when human migrations took place and people of the Indo-European stock migrated to the fertile oases of Samarkand, Tashkent, Bukhara and Merv. Some people occupied areas in the Fergana Valley, and their decendants, the *Sythians* were fine archmen and valliant fighters. They were skilled artisans who specialized in making gold jewellery and bows and arrows of bronze and iron.

Cyrus the Great, king emperor of Iran, subjugated them and those who lived on the banks of river Zerafshan were called

Sogdiana who later played an important role as traders on the Silk Route; they were famous wood carvers and carpet makers.

The Silk Route

The Chinese have been famous silk producers since the ancient times, much before the Christian era, but its export was forbidden. During the period 138 BC-AD 484, China was subjected to frequent attacks on its northern frontier by the Mongol (Hsuing Nu) nomads. So the Chinese emperor Wu-ti sent his army General Chang Chie in 138BC to buy the world famous horses from Central Asia to strengthen the armed constabulry (Today Turkmenistan enjoys world fame in horse breeding). From Kashgar Chang Chien crossed Tien Shan and reached Fergana. It was here that Chang Chien came to know that Sodgian merchants would pay a handsome price for silk. The king emperor of China, Wu-ti, on hearing the high selling prices of silk, lifted the ban on silk for foreign markets. However, the threat of Mongol nomads was not over, although the route, which came to be known as the Silk Route was initiated.

It should be noted that the Silk Route is not one straight road but a network of roadways. Emanating from China, the route skirts Tarim Basin north and south.

Tarim Basin (Takla Makan) is a desert and to its north lies Sinkiang Range and the Tien Shan and in the south lies the Altyn Tagh Range and they meet at Kashgar at one end and Dushanbe at the other. One route then follows Amu Darya and the other follows Syr Darya and passing through northern Caspian it enters southern Russia. The route most frequently adopted was Kizyl Kum and Kara Kum deserts to Iran and before it enters Iran the route touches Samarkand, Bukhara and Merv and finally goes up to Rome, where the Chinese merchants sold silk, spices, arms, jade and mirror and purchased coral, glass, textiles, pottery, gold and silver. Travelling on the Silk Route from China to Rome involved a couple of months.

From the middle of 5th century to the middle of 7th century AD (two hundred years) Huns and Turks invaded Central Asia. The Huns and the Sassanians established their empire but subsequently the Turks drove the Huns out by AD560. What was there in Central Asia which attracted the Huns and Turks? The Huns and Turks were great warriors. The limitless steppe grasslands attracted their attention and the Silk Route showed them the possibility of good trade between them and the Byzentine emperor. Then came the Arabs. The Sassanian empire was demolished and their last ruler was killed in Merv in 651, the Arabs established their headgmony for three hundred and fifty years from 651-992 AD. They captured Tashkent, Fergana, Samarkand and Bukhara[1] and left their imprint in the form of famous beautiful monuments, particularly the mausoleum, mosques and madarsas.[2]

Alexander the Great in BC329 said about Samarkand "Everything I have heard about beauty of Saarkand is true, except that it is more beautiful than I could have imagined".

With the discovery of the Silk Route, the prosperity of Samarkand further increased. Silk in European markets fetched high prices. However, with the arrival of Seljuks (992-1150) the hold of Huns declined. The Arabs captured Bukhara, Samarkand and Tashkent. Bukhara became a centre of Islamic learning and finely built mausoleums here, stands as a testimony to Bukhara's grandeur in the tenth century AD.

The top left in Plate 3 depicts the concept of the Madrasa as an institution separate from the mosque first developed in Central Asia.

The top left shows the courtyard Sher Dar Madarsa in Samarkand showing one of the diwan. Teachers and students lived in the halls around the court as they might in Oxford and Cambridge.

From 1150 to 1370, the Mongol invasion brought great devastation to Central Asia. Genghis Khan (1167-1227) had welded the Mongols into a formidable fighting force. Iran was conquered and many Iranian cities were destroyed. China was

Plate 3

Monumental Gateway of a Madrass in Samar Kand Built Between 1619-1616 (Central Asia). The Gateway is Decorated with Coloured Tiles

Source: Robinson Francis (1982), *Atlas of the Islamic World Since 1500*, London.

conquered. Baghdad was sacked and the Mongol armies reached southern Russia, Hungary and even touched the Adriatic. As the Mongols could not hold so vast an area, they founded an autocracy known as the Golden Horde, which dominated southern and European Russia for 200 years. The period in Central Asia between 1370 and 1500, belongs to Tamerlane. Tamerlane lived between 1335 and 1405. He belonged to Turkestan. Timur, the lame, conquered the territory north of Amu Darya and east of Caspian Sea and made Samarkand his capital. He conquered Iran, defeated the army of the Golden Horde, destroyed Baghdad, Aleppo and Damascus. He wanted to conquer China but could not succeed.

Then, in Central Asia came the Uzbek Khanates (1500-1717) and the modern Uzbek's ancestors were Mongols. Under Mohammad Sheibanid they crossed Syr Daya in 1500. One batch of Sheibanid dynasty founded the Khanate of Khiva. Another of their rulers, Abdullah Khan commissioned some of Bukhara's finest mosques and extended the Khanate rule east of Kashgar and north of Tashkent.[3]

The Russians arrived on the scene and from 1717 to 1917, they made their inroads and established themselves. In 1917 the Russian Revolution took place and Central Asia came within the ambit of Russia (the former USSR). As Central Asia became part of USSR, the lands of Central Asia reorganized into various states, for example, the Kara Kum desert and part of Amu Darya delta became Turkistan; land surrounding Bukhara between the Amu Darya, Samarkand and Tashkent became Uzbekistan; part of the Fergana mountain north of Alai range became Kyrgyzstan. Valley and Pamirs and some other enclaves became Tajikistan, and the mountain north of Alai range became Kyrgyzstan, In 1936, Kazakhstan was separated from the Russian Federation and constituted as a state under Soviet Union.

Purging in the central Soviet states started in a big way. Persons subscribing to communist ideology were put in high positions and those subscribing to religious beliefs were ignored. The Cyrilic (Russian) alphabets replaced Arabic. Russian language became compulsory in schools and all the 26,000 mosques, expect 400, were closed. However, the Russian rule benefited the economy. The Five-Year Plans were applied for the development of resources. Irrigation was expanded on a big scale and large parts of the desert were turned into smiling fields (though it was at the cost of environment) and Central Asia became one of the leading producers of cotton. The virgin lands were brought under wheat cultivation in a big way. Large areas were put under corn cultivation to provide fodder for the animals. Exploitation of oil and gas resources improved the economic conditions of the region, but there was considerable resistance to Russian rule.

It was in 1991, that the dissolution of USSR came into being. Instead of Central planned economy, it was suggested that market forces should determine the means of production. Private enterprise be encouraged and instead of regimentation, there should be democracy. Fears were voiced in American and British quarters that Islamic fundamentalism might grip these states, but fortunately all the states which were declared independent announced secularism as the cardinal principle of state policy. All the Central Asian states became members of the Commonwealth of Independent States (CIS) and also members of the International Monetary Fund (IMF).

The official language in Tajikistan became Persian. The Islamic regime of Taliban cast its shadow on Tajikistan and since independence conflict has arisen between the secular forces of the government and the opposition. Several thousand people have been killed and several thousands migrated to Afghanistan as refugees. In fact relations with Afghanistan were strained by the apparent inability of the Afghan government to prevent *Mujahidin* fighters and the dispatch of arms from crossing the frontier into Tajikistan. However, the Afghan government has denied that it was involved in the traffic of arms. There are about 16,500 border guards (mainly Russian) keeping a vigil on outside invasions.

Nuclear Pile

It would be worthwhile to mention that the vast open land in northern Kazakhstan attracted attention of the erstwhile Soviet Union to carry on nuclear experiments and make a stockpile of nuclear armaments. On being independent, Kazakhstan inherited this legacy and today it is the fourth nuclear power in the world. Semiplatinsk became the centre of the test sites and the Russians space rockets went under experiments from the Baikonur Cosmodrome.

NASA charged $ 70 million to plant a satellite in orbit while Baikonur does it for $ 1.5 million. Up till 1991 the place was closely guarded, but now the cosmodrome is open, with certain conditions to the public. The launch site cosmodrome is near the military city of Leninsk, on the Syr Darya, 250 km away from Kzyl Orda. The village Baikonur is 300 km north of the launch site and has nothing to do with space travel.

The space programme still runs and is funded by Russia and mission control is still at star city outside Moscow. Kazakhstan has announced that it would not make any nuclear experiments since the cosmodrome is on sovereign territory of Kazakhstan, permission to go there must be obtained from Kazakhstan.

There is no public airport at Leninsk. The nearest airport is at Kzyl Orda or from Kzyl Orda one can reach Leninsk in four hours by road or six hours by train.[4]

Notes

1. Whittell, Giles, *Central Asia: Cadogan Guides: The Practical Handbook*, London, p. 108.
2. Madrasa refers to educational institution where the teaching is conducted in the oriental style. The Madrasa was the typical building of the age and it was developed as an institution separate from the mosque.
3. Source: *Atlas of the Islamic World, Since 1500*, London,1982.

4. Whittell Giles (1993), *Central Asia: Cadogan Guides: The Practical Handbook*, London, p. 52.
5. Whittell Giles (1993), *Central Asia: Cadogan Guides: The Practical Handbook*, London, pp. 224-45.

9

Culture of Central Asia

Culture is a complex term and it is not fixed for all times to come. It is much influenced by technological development, and the scientific and technological development bring about a social change.

Environmental factors in the early stages of development of a society profoundly influence the building material, food, clothing, shelter, art, architecture, language and literature and certain special characteristics are evolved, over a period of time, which distinguish one region from another. These regional characteristics become the distinguishing hallmark of a region.

The type of food which the people eat is generally derived from the region where the people live. People living near the coast include fish as the principal item of their diet, and if the region receives heavy rainfall, and has warm to hot summer it may produce rice, the diet of the people in that region shall generally be based on rice and fish, but if the area is fertile, and receives annual rainfall less then 50 cm, and possesses adequate irrigation facilities it may grow wheat. Wheat bread then feature as the principal item of diet. However, if the rainfall is low with inadequate arrangement of irrigation, the region will generally grow millet. Thus, in the absences of high technological development, the breakfast table in a region of high rainfall may serve rice and in many cases fish also, while the low rainfall area may have millet or gram with some vegetables and the two regions would present a contrast in their culture.

The adjustment of each society to the peculiarities of the local physical environment, taking place over many centuries, produce local characteristics in that society which are not to be found elsewhere and humans and nature become moulded to one another over the years. The influences of man and nature on each other form a sort of an amalgam and give a special characteristic by which the region is usually designated. The characteristics are accumulated over the years giving the region a 'local' and 'rural' characteristic: local in the sense that the bulk of the material for building, for food, for fuel, and in the manufacture of implements should be of local origin. It will give rise to typical regional food, particular art and architecture, and dialect and literature. It shall be rural in the sense that the population shall be working on the land or serving those on the land.[1]

These processes apply as long the region has not undergone technological revolution, but with the onset of industrial revolution, most of the special traits disappear with the dissolution of traditional, rural, local and regional pattern of life, resulting in the emergence of a new social order. The new society produces goods on a large-scale, which are cheap and easily available. Food, clothing, building material and implement cease to be locally made and the traditional characteristics gradually disappear. It should however, be noted that these changes do not come overnight, nor do they affect all areas equally or quickly. The means of transport become so efficient that the goods being produced several thousand kilometres away are available in one's home area. It follows from the situation that the process leaves us all dependent upon a network of communications covering the whole earth.

The cultural pattern in a region changes and a social change takes place when the relationships among groups of people are modified and cultural changes may lead to social changes. Values, laws, and customs are as important for cultural creation as technology. Out of society comes culture.

If society changes, culture would also change. New norms are framed, since the old norms no longer serve the purpose.

Change within Social Systems

Social systems are fields of tension in which dissatisfactions are produced and improvements are sought. Social and cultural changes occur when novel patterns of sought and action arise in the organization of a group and the appearances of novelty is innovation.

Innovation may occur through two different processes. It may come about through invention or it may be brought about through the interaction of the people as they respond to each other's expectations. The interactions are communicated from the place of origin to other groups through the process of diffusion.

Cultural Profile of Central Asia

Central Asia (the five states Kazakhstan, Turkmenistan, Uzbekistan, Tajikistan and Kyrgyzstan) occupy 3,996,400 sq km, almost half the area of USA, the states range in size from Kazakhstan with an area of 2,717,300 sq km to Tajikistan with 143,100 sq km with more than 58 million people (2001). In all the states taken together Uzbekistan has the largest population followed by Kazakhstan, Tajikistan, Kyrgyzstan, and Turkmenistan. Population density throughout the region varies widely from an average of 52.1 persons per sq km in Uzbekistan to about 10 person per sq km in Turkmenistan.

The arid and semi-arid climate contributes to the uneven population distribution pattern of Central Asia. Most of the people of the region are concentrated along the banks of the major river systems and their tributaries, also in the foothills of the mountains in the south and south-east and in the oases.

About 60 per cent of Central Asia is desert. The principal sand deserts are the Karakum (black sand) which occupies most of the territory of Turkmenistan and the Kyzylkum (red sand) which covers most of Uzbekistan.

As all the states resemble in their physical characteristics and climate, the cultural characteristics are by and large similar. There is great similarity in language. Most of the languages spoken in Central Asia are related to the Turkish language and are part of the Turkie group of languages. The major exception is Tajik which is part of the Iranian group of languages.[2]

Turkie, Tibetan, Mongol and Persian are the important languages in Central Asia which have developed literature. The Turkish literature in Central Asia developed mostly up to seventh century before the conversion of Central Asian tribes to Islam. The early Turkie literature relates epics and in forceful language describes the origin of Turks, their golden age, their subjugation by the Chinese, and their subsequent liberation.

Tibetan language has been developed in Central Asian countries, as a result of their cultural contact with India and other Buddhist countries. Central Asian states had contact with north-western India (Kashmir and Kulu) and Nepal. Scripts of Indian origin were in use in these countries, so the Tibetans also adopted an Indian script to suit their own language. Most of the work produced in the Central Asian states between the seventh and thirteenth centuries were translations of Buddhist works, largely from Sanskirt on which Indian scholars and Tibetan translators worked side by side. There is considerable Indian influence on the evolution of Tibetan language, particularly sophisticated vocabulary expressing many ideas for which new terms had to be coined.

Nomadic Culture

Central Asia experiences a continental climate. It is characterized by high summer temperature, cold winters and very low precipitation. In the lowlands the annual rainfall varies between 10 and 25 cm. The steppes extend in an uninterrupted belt from the shores of the eastern Caspian Sea to the foothills of Altay mountains. This includes the principal desert, the Karakum occupying most of Turkmenistan, and the Kyzlkum which covers nearly all of Uzbekistan. In the east and south there are a number of mountains: the Kopet Dag, in the south bordering northern Iran, the Hindu Kush in the south bordering northern Afghanistan, the Pamirs occupying most of Tajikistan in the south and Tien Shah extending eastwards to China.

Climate and scanty rainfall conspired to make nomadism as the chief occupation of the people during the first millennium BC and the early centuries of the Christian era. Settled agriculture with large-scale irrigation converting virgin lands into smiling fields with environmental consequences is a recent phenomenon. It is rather surprising that even before the Christian era, certain nomadic tribes made history by producing works of art.

From the beginning of the recorded history, pastoral nomadism has been practised in Central Asia on a very large scale. The horse was the chief instrument of waging war as well as for defence and the mounted archer was far superior to the foot soldier.

The economy and culture of Central Asian states were based on nomadism for over a thousand years. Huge herds of cattle were driven from place to place to make use of the pastures. In winters they fed on the grass of the lowlands where there was no snow, and the pastures which were available along the rivers. In the summer months, the herds of sheep were driven to fresh grasslands or towards the alpine pastures in the mountains. The nomads, particularly the Kazakhs travelled about a thousand kilometres each year with their flocks.

The nomads, in heat and in cold, lived in their beehive shaped felt tents stretched over a wooden frame. There was a hole at the top to let out smoke from the fire of dried dung that burned on the ground in the centre of the tent.[3] such was the life of the nomads of Central Asia. The sheep, goats, horses and the camels were their assets and they provided them milk, butter and cheese as they did not know bread and flour. They wanted new pastures for their flocks but they had ample free time. One of the important nomadic tribe of Central Asia was the Saka tribes which grazed their herds in the Pamirs, Central Tien Shan and the Amu Darya delta. The Saka nomads were highly artistic and as early as 530 BC, they tattooed designs on the male body. It has been discovered in Kurgan. The designs are also discovered on the human body, on the left shoulder and right leg. These designs have been found on the Scythians, a nomadic tribe living in the Cuban Basin of the Caucasus region in the first millennium BC.[4] Such tattooed designs have also been discovered from the burial sites of the western Altay mountains.

Tattooing was a common practice among the nomadic tribes and apart from human beings, the bodies of horses, woollen carpets and woven Persian fabrics had designs of riders, stags, and griffins.[5] These excavations were made at Pazyryk burial sites. Clothings made of felt, leather or fur were lavishly ornamented. Decorative art had a special place in the cultural life of people of Central Asia. Apart from beautiful shapes of birds and animals in tatooing, there can be seen a clear cultural influence of India on the decorative art of Central Asia as exhibited in the textile designs, hard-stone carvings and metal work in the early years of the Christian era before the advent of Moghals in India. Metal casting techniques in Central Asia came from India where the technique had reached an extraordinary level of sophistication, both technically and ethnically. Central Asian influences were more pronounced on the arts of India with the advent of Moghals. Luxury metal work (bidri of Deccan in India) attained a great reputation in India. Enameling and metal engraving which existed in India in the 17th century, reached its perfection under the Central Asian influences. Jade carving which was popular at the Moghal courts received its material from Khotin on the Dneister, close to Central Asia. Several jade carvings paved the way in India for the use of inlaid precious stones.

Architecture

The most notable and profound influence of Central Asia was felt in the middle ages on the architecture of buildings particularly on the mosque and tombs. Masonry arches, domes and vaults, presentation of decorative themes through calligraphy were the hallmark of buildings in India in the middle ages, and carried the influence of Central Asia.

Tomb architecture in Delhi and Agra consists usually of a single square domed chamber. Thick walls getting thinner upwards were decorated with an arched niche (mehrab) and carving of sculptured calligraphy were made on them in the Deccan. There were stylistic variants at Gulburga, the Jama Masjid was completely roofed over with domed and vaulted bays. At Bidar the theological college (madarsa) was purely Central Asian in form, completely with corner minarates, bulbous domes and coloured tiles. At Bijapur, the Gol Gumbad has one of the largest domes in the world and this has been ingeniously supported on a net of interesting pointed arches.

Central Asian influences on Indian architecture reached its high watermark under Moghul patronage in the sixteenth and seventeenth centuries. The Jama Masjid at Delhi, Agra and Fatepur Sikri have been constructed in red sandstone and white marble. The large courts of these mosques have monumental gates provided with highly ornamental arched doorways. Prayer chambers on the western side of the courts were sumptuously ornamented, walls, arches and domes have been carved in relief also inset with different coloured stones.

One of the greatest influences of Central Asian architecture was on the tomb garden in India and this was brought to a peak of perfection unknown elsewhere in the Islamic World. In such cases, the domed tomb is set within a garden regularly divided by paths and water courses into plots. The most popular garden scheme had four squares with the tomb in the middle as in the mausoleum of Humayun and Akbar at Delhi and Sikandra respectively.[6]

Shah Jahan's mausoleum for his wife at Agra known as Taj Mahal, has placed the tomb at one end; detached minarets were added at four corners. The domes were raised on cylindrical drums and were slightly bulbous in profile. Calligraphy and geometric ornament, often in polychrome stonework, covered the principal facades; and the interiors were dominated by great domes that rose over the cenotaphs. The Taj Mahal, executed entirely in white marble, is the masterpiece of the series. Its overall design is characterized by a striking simplicity and yet the ornamental treatment is superb. Even temple architecture has been influenced by this style, so much so that the celebrated Sikh sanctuary at Amritsar, the Golden Temple, shows influences from later Mughal architecture.[7]

Samarkand is a city famous for the grandeur of its mosques and madarsas. Among the mosques Bibi Khanym mosques and Shah-i-Zinda ensemble are most famous. It is 15th century mosque with a gate about 30 m high and its dome is even higher in height. There is a minaret at each corner. An earthquake in the 17th century destroyed half of the mosque and in the late 19th century cracks developed in the dome. Repair work on a big scale has been undertaken.

Uzbekistan is a land of mosques, museums, tombs and mausoleums. Ulug Bek Madrasa (seminary) is decorated with a mosaic of stars over its portico. Every other square inch of its exterior is covered in mosaic, spirals up the pillars and bands of Kufi calligraphy round the inside of the high vaulted arched, and geometric patterns resembling computer graphics on the facade are marked with grandeur in system.

Kalyan mosque in Bukhara is a fine example of dome architecture. There are 288 domes resting on an equal number of columns and form a courtyard 127 m long and 78 m wide and can accommodate more then 10,000 people.

The Uzbek cultural heritage includes magnificent monuments in the national architectural tradition. The mausoleum of the Samanid rulers Ismail I and his successors (9th and 10th centuries in Bukhara), the great mosques and mausoleums of Samarkand, constructed in the 14th and 15th centuries and many other fine tombs, mosques and palaces are fine examples of Central Asian architecture.

Painting

Painting was well developed in Central Asia and Moghal rulers in India from the twelfth to seventeenth centuries considerably encouraged this form of art. The earliest manuscripts, from the 11th century onwards were on palm leaf but from the late 14th century paper introduced by Muslims from Central Asia was increasingly used. Painting inspired by the reign of Akbar (1556-1605) and his successors brought about revolutionary changes in painting and the tradition continued up to the nineteenth century. Painting inspired by the Central Asian tradition were greatly patronized by the Moghal rulers. Babar, founder of the Moghal rule encouraged original paintings while Humayun (1530-56) was inspired by the exquisite paintings of the Safavid painters. Akbar promoted the art of painting by establishing a large studio of artists from every nook and corner of India who worked under the famous Safavid masters. Akbar himself supervised the making of these paintings. Thus, based on Central Asian traditions and the dynamic illustrative Persian style and technique, and the Indian workmanship together with western naturalism which reached the court of Akbar, about 1,400 large cloth paintings depicting the adventure story cycles (Hamzanama) was completed in about fifteen years (1562-1577). One of Akbar's monumental initiative was to get complete accomplished illustrated manuscript in Persian, of Hindu religious epic and also the official histories of his reign and the lives of the Timurid ancestors. The Akbarnama contains beautiful paintings showing crowded scenes of people at court, and painting of hunting and of battlefield.

A new change in the art of painting emerged in the light of Islamic teachings which prohibited the depiction of living beings. There was a revolution in the Indian painting with borrowed concept from Central Asia with its secular viewpoints and dispassionate observation of the world. Jehangir (1605-1627) made the Imperial studio, the place for the best artists of the country and focused attention on the preparation of individual pictures, instead of crowded scenes as preferred by his father. The artists would accompany the king in court or camp and would make a portrait of birds, animals and flowers pointed out by the king.

Thus, the focus of Mughal art which drew inspiration from the Savavid painters changed from large-scale scenes of crowded people to beautiful portraits of courtiers standing singly against a plain coloured background. Jehangir was a great secularist and encouraged outstanding artists (Hindus and Muslims) and conferred on them titles.

Shahjahan in the seventeenth century (1627-58) loved court pomp and embellished paintings, while during Aurangzeb's time from middle of seventeenth to early eighteenth century (1658-1707) paintings continued to flourish up to 1680, after which the King's interest declined in paintings and painters were transferred to regional courts. Standards of painting declined and the themes were confined to conventional topics and those related to *Harem*. In the middle of the eighteenth century the scene of artists shifted from Delhi to Avadh and Bengal. A new innovation in painting took place with the introduction of European tradition with the stronger grip of British on northern India.

In southern India during the middle of the sixteenth century painting was developed on the Persian and Turkish style with mixed Indian influences. Paintings of the Deccan were rich in colour, and their quality was exceptionally good. Ahmadnagar and Bijapur were important centres and Golkunda also became an important centre. Hyderabad in the middle of eighteenth century imbibed the Moghal traditions in painting.

Many important centres of paintings sprang up in the Moghal period at Rajput courts of Rajasthan, Central India and in Punjab and modern Himachal Pradesh. In Rajasthan, such centres were at Bundi, Kota and Udaipur, Amber (now Jaipur) and Jodhpur. The Maharaja's of princely states acquired a taste for paintings and revitalized the indigenous traditions. At Kishangarh, the paintings depicted scenes of eternal love sports of Lord Krishna and Radha. However, there came a general decline in painting after the mid-nineteenth century under the British influence. (In recent times mention may be made of the celebrated artist painter M.F.Husain, whose paintings vary from a modified social realism to abstract work). Thus, there was a powerful influence of Central Asia on Indian art and painting.

Dress

The general dress worn by people of Central Asia has the following basic style: tunic like shirts, wide trousers, oriental robes, embroidered skull caps, turbans or fur hats. Women wore wide dresses with a tight fitting top, coloured ornaments, the various types of kerchiefs, the designs of the fabrics varying with the region.

Some people wore quilted jackets (*beshmat*) with high collars, while some women wore a long dress, taken in at the waist which had a wide skirt embroidered in silver thread wool or silk.

In Kazakhstan, there is a sizeable Russian population and sometime they wear embroidered garments and leather boots. The Russian women wear long chemise and panel skirt open on the sides.

However, a great change has taken place and the people, particularly in the urban areas, now wear the western style dresses.

Food

Much of the food consumed by the rural and most of the urban population consists of salted and pickled vegetables, mushrooms and berries. Garlic, onions and saffron serve as spices. Cabbage is most commonly used including *golubtsy* which is stuffed cabbage rolls. Soups are an essential part of their diet. Most of the soups are made of beet root, cabbage, meat and vegetables. Some foods are made of pickled cucumbers. Cooked buckwheat, millet and barely and dark bread made either of buckwheat or barely are a regular item in their diet. The cooking medium is sunflower oil and sour cream but not butter. Patties with different fillings are counterpart of hamburger of USA. Fish is often an item of the diet. Tea is preferred over coffee and is taken in glasses with a metal holder.[8]

A variety of meat dishes play an important part in the cuisine of Central Asia. Very often the entire family or male members with guests sit together and a roast lamb shall be placed in the centre and boiled rice mixed with meat and clarified butter or sunflower oil is also served.

In India the cuisine shows Iranian and Central Asian influences. The food in northern India is often called as *mughlai* dishes having Lucknow and Delhi as their major centres. However, there is practically no influence of Central Asian food both in southern and eastern India.

Food in Central Asia is undergoing a social change, with the spread of education, means of communication and exchange of ideas through travelling.

Languages

There is not one single official language of all the Central Asian states. The official language of each state is different from the other. In Turkmenistan, about three-fourths of the population consists of Turkmen and Russians account for only one-tenth. So, in 1990, Turkman was declared the official language of the

Republic, and Turkman derives its origin from the Turkie group of languages.

Till 1929 the script was Arabic. The Arabic script was replaced by a Latin script. The Latin script was replaced by Cyrillic script in 1940. In 1993, the Republic announced to gradually change to a Latin based Turkish script.

In Uzbekistan, about three-fourths of the population consists of Uzbeks. Of the total population of 24 million, Uzbeks constitute about 17 million and about 2 million are Russians. The official language is Uzbek. The script since 1940 has been Cyrillic and it will gradually revert to the Latin script.

In Tajikistan, of the total population of 15.4 million, more than 60 per cent are Tajik and about 25 per cent are Uzbeks. The official language is Tajik.

In Kyrgyzstan, of the total population of 5.2 million, a little more than half consist of Kyrgyz, and one-fifth are Russians and about one-sixth are Uzbeks. So, the official languages are Kyrgyz and Russian.

In Kazakhstan of the total population of about 15.4 million, the Kazakhs are 45 per cent and Russians are 36 per cent.[9] Then, there are Ukranians, Germans and Uzbeks which make up 11 per cent. The official language is Kazak.

Although the official language of one state is different from the other, all the states (CIS) and as the Central Asian states having been a part of the erstwhile Soviet Union, Russian language is understood in all the states and constitutes the vehicle of intercommunication.

Russian, both literary and spoken is a rich and flexible language. There are 33 letters in the Russian alphabet and they represent all the sounds which in other languages must be formed by a combination of two or more letter.

Literature

Central Asian states up to 1990 were a part of the erstwhile Soviet Union. The general development of Russian literature should be considered as a heritage of Central Asian states.

Russian literature refers to imaginative literature produced in the erstwhile Soviet Union from 1917 to the present day Russia. The Bolshevik Revolution and the transformation of Russian society, which followed, created radically different conditions for the emergence of new literature.

Russian literature can be considered in three groups:

1. The period of relative liberalism, i.e., 1917-1932.
2. The period of socialist realism, i.e., 1932-1935.
3. From 1953 after the death of Stalin to the present date.

Prior to the Revolution, Russia produced some very great poets, writers and novelists. The first to excite real interest in romanticism is A.S. Pushkin (1799-1837). He is author of the first Russian National Drama, *Boris Godunov* in which under the influence of Shakespeare, he abandoned the three unities (time, place and action). A hundred years after his death, his lyrics are still inimitable in their unity of content and form.

Another writer of the 19th century who kept alive the traditional Russian faith in a higher sphere of reality, to which one might aspire in vision and in dreams, is Dostoyevsky. His books: *Crime and Punishment, The Idiot, The Brothers Karamezov* represent stages in the development of the psychological and the philosophical novel. L.S. Tolstoy (1828-1910) wrote his prose epic of the Napoleonic wars *War and Peace*, and *Anna Karenina*. His endless quest for freedom, for truth, for simplicity found a most adequate expression in his writings.

Other writers who appeared at the time on the literary scene are A.P. Chekhov, Bunin and Maxim Gorky. Chekhov's non-humorous short stories as *My Life, Steppe, The Duel,* reveal him as a great writer, artist with universal appeal. His plays *Three Sisters, The Cherry Orchard*, were written in the same appealing style. I.A. Bunin (1870-1953) wrote lucid and lyrical prose. He wrote in a superb style and his book *The Village* is remarkable for it exquisite system and power of observation. He was awarded Noble Prize in 1933. Maxim Gorky (1868-1936), wrote about crude, harsh realities, poverty sickness and death.[10] The Russian writers provided suitable academic climate which induced Central Asian writers to excel in diverse academic fields.

Central Asia produced many eminent persons who wrote world famous accounts of their travels, scientific findings, and in the field of geology, astronomy, mineralogy, medicine. Important names that can be mentioned are those of Al Beruni, Al Idrisi, Al Razi, Avicina and Ibne Khatdoon. Al Beruni, whose full name was Mohammad Abu Rahan Al Beruni passed his youth on the banks of Syr Darya in the city of Khwarizm. He has written a large number of books and has dwelt upon a great variety of subjects. His book Patanjali in Sanskrit, translated into Arabic, contains valuable information on India and Asia. He wrote on philosophy, mathematics, chronology, medicine, astronomy, geology, geomorphology and mineralogy.

A number of modern Tajik poets and novelists achieved fame even before independence of Tajikistan. Abdalrauf Fitrat whose *Last Judgment* has been reprinted many times in Tajik, Uzbek and Russian. He is a famous writer of Central Asia.

The Kyrgyz take pride in Chingiz Ayt-Matov a novelist and story writer who wrote mainly in Russian but also in Kyrgyz. His Taboo *of Mountains and Steppes* and the more recent *A Day Lasts More Than a Hundred Years* received wide circulation in Russian and English translations. Aytmatov's play *The Ascent of Mt. Fuji* written by Kazakh playwright Kaltay, M, discusses openly the moral compromises made under the Stalin regime. This play caused a sensation when it was staged in Moscow in 1973.

Mention should be made of the following outstanding persons who through their writings and researches brought great fame to Central Asia.

Avicena: Abu Ali Al Husain Ibn Abdullah Ibn Sina (980-1037). He was born in a village in Bukhara. Avicena's large philosophical encyclopaedia is *Ash Shifa*. Called *An Najat* (the salvation) became popular and was printed as an appendix to *Al*

Qanun in 1593. Avicena's monumental work is *Isharat wa Tanbihat* (Demonstrations and Affirmation). This book covers his whole philosophy and represents his most mature thoughts.

His most famous medical work is *Al Qaunun Fil Tib* (The Canon of Medicine), a systematic encyclopedia for the most part on Greek and Arabic works.

This work not only became extremely popular in the Islamic world, but was also studied in European Universities for centuries. It was printed 15 times before 1500.

Omar Khayyam: Omar Ibn Ibrahim Al Khayyam, though born in Nishapur, maintained close contact with Central Asian states. He was an eminent mathematician, astronomer and free thinker. His standard work in Algebra, written in Arabic raised him to the foremost rank among the mathematicians of that age. He was called by Sultan Malik Shah in AD 1074, to institute astronomical observations on a large scale and suggest a thorough reform of the calendar. He revised the astronomical tables. His poetical renown is acclaimed universally The *Rubiyat* or quotations, constitute a collection of 500 epigrams.

The *Rubiyat* are the expressions of wisdom of a radical thinker, who protests in the most forceful manner both against the narrowness, bigotry and uncompromising austerity of the orthodox. *Ulema* and the eccentricity, hypocrisy and ravings of advanced *Sufis*.[11]

Ulugh Beg, who lived in the 15th century, was an eminent astronomer and mathematician. He founded a famous observatory in Samarkand. Al Shir Nava I greatly advanced Turkie language and literature and was a talented artist and composer.

Over the centuries, Uzbekistan has produced great scholars, poets and writers whose heritage has enriched the general culture of humanity. In the early twentieth century, the foremost modern poets and prose writers included.

Abdal Rauf Fitrat Sadruddin Ayni and Abdullah Qadiri who were bilingual in Uzbek and Tajik, wrote plays, stories and novels on Central Asia.

The second half of the 20th century saw a great increase in the number of writers but not in the quality of writing. Until the 1980s most Uzbek authors produced novels and plays on the lines of official communist party themes.

Music

Russian musical art was introduced in the first decade of the 20th century, although musical instruments had been in general use from the earliest times of Russian history. Some of the musical instruments are: Gudok, a bow instrument, Gusli, small horn, pipes, the drums, kettle drums and tambourines. The musicians played at festival occasions. Musorgsky (1839-81) was one of Russian's most important composers. The Russian music society was established in 1859 to advance the development of music and education and to encourage local talents.

Chanaber music was popular in Russia from the end of the eighteenth century. Early into thirteenth century, Chanaber music recitals were fairly common in large cities. In the past 60 years, hundreds of operas, thousands of orchestra works and many thousands of folk songs and romances have been published in Russia. A good deal of music is written by regional composers, natives of Georgia, Armenia, Azerbaijan and Uzbekistan. The Soviet ballet is known for outstanding dancers such as Galina Ulonova and some excellent music composers.

Notes

1. Wrighey, E.A. (1965), "Changes in the Philosophy of Geography" in *Frontier in Geographical Teaching*, London, pp. 8-9.
2. *Encyclopedia Britannica*, pp. 701 and 716.
3. Mikhailov, N., *Soviet Russia*, New York, 1948, p. 268.
4. *Encyclopedia Britanica*, p. 725.
5. Griffins are imaginary animals with lion's body and eagle's beak and wings.

6. Robinson, Francis (1989), *The Cambridge Encyclopedia of India*, Cambridge, pp. 459-461.
7. Ibid., p. 461.
8. Florinskhy, Michael T., (1961) *Encyclopedia of Russia and the Soviet Union*, London, p. 479.
9. The population of Kazakhs in Kazakhstan has recently increased to 53 per cent.
10. Florinsky, M.T., (1961) *Encyclopedia of Russia and the Soviet Union*, London, pp. 314-316.
11. *Encyclopedia Britanica*, Vol. 16.

10

Central Asia: Problems and Prospects

Many problems which the Central Asian States (CAS) face today have their origin in the climate. The five states of Central Asia, which became Independent Republics after 1990, cover a vast area of about 4 million sq km (3,986,400 sq km), extending from the Caspian Sea in the west to the Chinese frontier in the east and from the borders of southern Siberia in the north to the borders of Iran and Afghanistan in the south.

Two-thirds of Central Asia in the north-western section consists of low sandy deserts interspersed by irrigated oases in the south-east and along the foothill of the mountains. Various types of deserts (sand, clay, salt and stone) and the Hungry Steppes occupy most of the area. In the extreme north and north-east the lands are called virgin lands. The two deserts Kara Kum and Kyzyl Kum, separated from each other by Amu Darya are fairly extensive. Kyzyl kum is a sandy desert, while Kara Kum has more rocky areas. In the south-east one-third of the total area is mountainous with highest glaciated ranges of the world.

The climate is characterized by extreme conditions – hot summers and cold winters while the valleys of mountains, like

Fergana and Zeravshan, the climate is mild. Over most of the area the amount of rainfall is 10 to 12 cm.

Agricultural development in Central Asia must be eco-friendly and the cultivation of crops should be compatible with the environment. However, it was in 1953, that in respect of agriculture of Central Asia (particularly of Kazakhstan), when it was part of erstwhile Soviet Union, an unprecedented event happened to boost production of cereals. This was the opening up of the new virgin lands in the dry steppe areas east of the river Volga. These lands could be converted to cultivable lands with little preparation. Within a span of four years, 40 million hectares of land, largely in northern Kazakhstan (and western Siberia) were put into cultivation for spring wheat.

In Kazakhstan, exclusively the area that was brought under cultivation was about 10 million hectares and by 1961 it rose to 28.6 million hectares. No soil survey was conducted and no assessment of the quality of soil was made. No detailed study of the availability of water was made. The average temperature in July in northern Kazakhstan is about 20°C and it receives up to 25 cm of rainfall in the April-October period. Short spring is followed by a long hot summer with temperatures often reaching 38°C to 40°C in the day time and dropping to a few degrees above freezing during night. The soils are brown with less then 2 per cent humus content and have greater salt content.[1] Table 39 shows the comparative yield per hectare of various crops of Central Asia and other countries of the world. The overall production did increase, but the yield per hectare was low with great variations from year to year. So it was a gamble against the weather.

Rice is a crop which consumes enormous quantities of water. Kazakhstan and Turkmenistan grow rice for which there is little justification. Rice could be substituted by pearl millet, a dry zone crop and an extension in its area would be eco-friendly as well. Millet is a rich source of protein, with unsaturated fats and minerals, as its yield in the Central Asian countries is low, method should be evolved to increase the yield per hectares by integrating biotechnology to evolve new varieties. India's yield of millet in 1960 was 367 kg per hectare but in 2000-03 it rose to 703 kg per hectare. In such hostile environment new varieties of millet would bring a ray of hope to farmers.

One is reminded of the bold experiment of the Groundnut Scheme in East Africa undertaken by the British government. Because of the world shortage of fats and oils, the British government decided to reclaim 1.3 million hectares (3.25 million acres) of almost uninhabited tropical Savanna land in East Africa for groundnut (peanut) production with the objective of quick return and a total yield of 600,000 tonnes of nuts a year. The report which was prepared by three experts, aimed at establishing 107 mechanized farm units of 12,000 hectares each, 80 in Tanganyika (modern Tanzania), 17 in Northern Rohodesia (Zambia) and 10 in Kenya. In 1947, the first year, 60,000 hectares were to be cleared and 180,000 hectares in 1948.

In the first year only 30,000 could be planted and the crop is said to have been less than the seed nuts put into the ground.[2]

In January 1951 complete failure was admitted. The loss at that time was £ 36 million of the British taxpayer's money.

The crux of the problem in Central Asia is that we need to know how to manage arid land soils. We need effective control of water supply; we need to produce nutritious grasses and strain of fodder crops such as the deep rooted alfalfa and clover so as to maintain a fodder supply throughout the year.[3]

Another innovation that was introduced from 1953-60 by the erstwhile Soviet Union was the corn growing programme and some of the best wheat lands were vacated and given to the growing of corn, as the growing of corn was considered as an answer to the meat problem in the country. A small area was given to ripe corn (7 million hectares) and 30 million hectares mostly virgin lands were brought under cultivation in north Kazakhstan, western Siberia, lower Volga and Ural for growing corn mainly for green fodder. The collective and the state farms

Table 39

Comparative Study Table 1994: Yield of Crops

(Yield per hectare in kg)

Countries	*Wheat*	*Rice*	*Coarse Grain*	*Barely*	*Maize*	*Rye*	*Oats*	*Millet*	*Sorg-hum*	*Roots & Tuber*	*Potatoes*	*Pulses*	*Sugar beet*	*Tobacco Leaves*	*Cotton Lints*
Kazakhstan	717	2775	887	909	1668	788	1274	358	1000	9742	9142	800	9978	1050	-
Kyrgyzstan	1835	1000	2033	1765	3243	3000	125000	-	1500	11520	11520	-	5500	2900	-
Tajikistan	917	1538	986	850	2091	1000	1000	-	750	10769	10796	800	-	2000	-
Turkmenistan	2298	3349	3505	2063	5008	1983	2190	1375	759	10000	10000	-	-	2000	75
Uzbekistan	1244	3257	1416	1164	2247	1500	1429	610	1250	12489	12489	-	19960	1600	4
China	3318	5869	4297	2286	5033	1140	1801	1667	3707	14968	12505	1338	-	4769	160
India	2420	2817	1016	1828	1750	-	-	703	977	15658	15000	607	-	1311	-
Japan	3718	6770	2926	3608	3485	-	2235	1745	-	25858	30057	1579	55201	2779	-
Korea Rep	2857	6083	3636	2444	4167	788	-	1200	1100	20031	20000	1193	-	2473	-
Egypt	5003	7915	6012	2083	6681	2000	-	-	4655	22231	21333	2130	46480	-	-
Denmark	6496	-	4968	4919	-	4742	6800	-	-	38530	38530	3765	54723	-	-
France	6676	4555	6411	5439	7827	3911	4127	2400	5513	32728	32728	5011	66507	2576	-
Italy	8989	5553	6500	3789	8362	2944	2544	-	5918	22847	22835	1732	44700	2344	-
Netherlands	8067	-	5497	5208	7164	4732	5073	-	-	45049	45049	4000	65789	-	-
Germany	6707	-	5103	5063	6821	4669	4600	-	-	31551	31551	2703	49426	1497	-
World	2445	3651	2717	2188	4330	2051	1708	689	1394	1303	14591	847	32775	1553	43

expanded their corn areas from 4 million hectares in 1953 to 28 million hectares in 1960 and a peak of 37 million hectares was reached in 1962.

The weather was not favourable in 1959 and crop production declined by 12 per cent and due to disastrous droughts in 1963, production further declined.

The result of all this was that the overall production of wheat declined and Soviet Union from a wheat exporting country became a wheat importing country in 1963, and in 1963-64 it imported 11 million tonnes of wheat.

Area under wheat cultivation in Kazakhstan from 1992 to 1994 varied between 12 and 13 million hectares but there was great fluctuation both in yield and production. The virgin land programme proved a flop and there was crisis in Russian agriculture (Table 40).

Table 40

Wheat Cultivation in Kazakhstan (1992-1994)

Year	*Yield (kg per hectare)*	*Production (in 000 MT)*
1992	1318	18285
1993	909	11585
1994	717	9052

Source: FAO Year Book *'Production'*, Vol. 50, 1996, Rome.

There is not so much fluctuation in the yield as well as production of wheat in Kyrgyzstan and Tajikistan. There is perceptible fluctuation in Uzbekistan but in Turkmenistan the fluctuation is significant.

In order to attain sustainability in agriculture, the pattern of crops must be eco-friendly. Whenever, man has violated this norm, there has been crisis in agriculture and a long-term degradation of land has taken place. There were many violations of the environment which led to the collapse and failure of the virgin land programme.

In the first instance, owing to cool short summers in western Siberia and northern Kazakhstan, only 20 per cent of the corn planted could mature into ripe grain.

Second, corn cut for silage and green fodder has often been in such immature stage that it has had little food value and the indiscriminate sowing of corn in many unsuitable regions had an adverse effect on agriculture. In many regions it served as green manure.

Where corn and winter wheat have been growing in rotation, farmers left the corn to ripen rather than to harvest it early enough to plant in the next year with wheat crop before winter set in. When sowing of winter wheat was delayed, yield of wheat declined.

The area under grasslands declined from 50 million hectares to 30 million hectares. These marginal lands were not suitable for corn.

During the decade 1953-63, the cultivation of oat's acreage declined from 16 million hectares to 6 million hectares in the Soviet Union. Rye in the same period declined from 21 million hectares to 16 million hectares. In fact, oats is a high protein cereal which is good feed grain for most livestock and it is well adapted for growing in cool moist areas.[4]

Land Use Survey

The cropping pattern should be evolved on the basis of a land use, land classification and land capability survey and such a survey be conducted with the help of remote sensing techniques and supplemented by ground surveys. In such a survey additional data be collected about the quality of soil on the basis of chemical analysis of sample soil surveys, availability of water for irrigation, the type and quantity of fertilizers available and methods of pest management. Land use maps be prepared, and the crops to be cultivated be marked on the maps. Such maps shall serve as permanent records for cropping pattern.

An environmental problem has been created in the Central Asian states owing to excessive irrigation. Extensive and intensive irrigation has converted large arid areas into smiling fields and has made Uzbekistan and Turkmenistan and Tajikistan as leading producers of cotton and Kazakhstan, Uzbekistan and Tajikistan produce substantial quantities of rice. Table 41 shows the cotton production and Table 42 shows production of rice in Central Asian states.

Table 41

Cotton Production

(in 000 metric tonnes)

	1993	*1994*	*1995*	*2000*	*2001*	*2002*
Uzbekistan	1306	1215	1306	1000	1015	1008
Turkmenistan	402	385	403	232.6	184.0	148.0
Tajikistan	150	151	135	93	145	113
Kazakhstan	76	60	50	95.5	112.7	90.4

Table 42

Rice Production

(in 000 metric tonnes)

	1993	*1994*	*1995*	*2000*	*2001*	*2002*
Uzbekistan	545	490	550	155	68	145
Kazakhstan	467	403	283	214.3	198.7	199
Turkmenistan	38	109	90	27.3	28.1	80
Tajikistan	23	20	20	82	40	29

Source: FAO Year Book *'Production'*, Vol. 50, 1996, Rome.

It will be seen that rice requires copious irrigation. Cotton also needs irrigation. The cultivation of rice in arid and semi-arid areas is not eco-friendly. Rice is a crop of humid zone. In hot and semi-arid areas it could be produced with heavy irrigation, but it will be an extravagant use of water and in the long run it will adversely affect the structure of soil, raise the subsoil water and lead to marshy conditions. Crop planning for Central Asian states is a must.

Central Asian States (CAS), today, are the leading producers of cotton. Cotton is a dry zone crop, but during the growing period it does require irrigation.

The scheme of bringing huge virgin lands under cultivation with the help of irrigation in northern Kazakhstan, and increasing the area under cultivation in Uzbekistan, Tajikistan and Turkmenistan, and rapid water withdrawal from Amu Darya, Syr Darya and their tributaries was enormous, so much so, that by 1965, 4.5 million hectares of Central Asia were irrigated and later on it rose to 7 million hectares. The withdrawal of water was so huge that Aral Sea, which in 1950 covered an area of 68,000 sq km containing 1,064 cubic km of water with a mean depth of 16 metres, shrank to 37 thousand sq km in 1989 and the volume of water in the Arsal Sea was reduced to 340 cubic km from 1,100 cubic km in 1960, and the total run-off into the sea was reduced from 40 cubic km to 5 cubic km.

Ecological Consequences

Aral Sea may become a small saltish lake of 4 to 5 thousand sq km. The Aral Sea has almost completely lost its productive fisheries. The human promoted desertification of the Aral and its region has also created health problems.

Agriculture is characterised by a predominance of one single crop – cotton. There is almost no crop rotation; also there is cultivation of water-intensive rice. The cultivation of marginal lands, yields low harvests and lead to abundant salt laden run-off.

The anthropogenic desertification of the Aral region must be stopped otherwise the Aral Sea will be replaced by a 60,000 sq km salt and sand desert generating dust that will harm the oases.[5]

In order to save the Aral Sea and Aral Sea region and the neighbouring oases from desertification, the cropping pattern in CAS should be reoriented and water intensive crop be replaced by crops of low water requirements. Sprinkler/drip irrigation should be introduced. Where surface irrigation is carried out, drainage should be improved and the surplus water be stored, desalinized and used for irrigation. In fact, CAS need sustainable development of agriculture. Sustainable agriculture refers to the use of resources in such a way as the needs and aspirations of the present generation are satisfied without compromising the needs of the future generations. In a land of scarce rainfall and high temperature, one may draw as much as is possible from the soil with the help of surface irrigation, without caring for drainage, structure of the soil, but soon a day would come when the soil would become completely sterile. What Kazakhstan, Turkmenistan and Tajikistan need today is to perfect the methods of dryland farming.

As much as 70 per cent of India's agriculture (net sown area) is rainfed. Crops grown and cropping patterns followed in these areas entirely depend on the rainfall which is often erratic and unpredictable. Bulk of these crops like jowar (big millet), bajara (bulrush millet), other coarse grain crops, pulses, oilseeds and cotton are grown in this area under rainfed conditions. India has made rapid strides in improving the methods of dryland farming particularly with reference to reducing the regional disparities between irrigated and vast unirrigated areas; restored ecological balance by greening rainfed areas through appropriate mixture of trees, shrubs and grasses, and has developed holistic approach for integrated farming system developed on watershed basis in rainfed areas. It would be worthwhile for CAS to seek cooperation with India in this respect.

Central Asian states are rich in petroleum and natural gas. Tables 43 to 46 show the production of crude petroleum and natural gas.

Table 43
Crude Petroleum Production

(in 000 metric tonnes)

	1992	*1993*	*1994*	*1995*	*1996*	*1997*
Kazakhstan	21795	19287	20289	20645	22937	25700
Kyrgyzstan	-	88	88	89	84	-
Tajikistan	57	39	32	64	-	-
Turkmenistan	-	-	3866	4400	4700	
(8 trillion cu.m.R)	-					
Uzbekistan	3943	3943	5517	5500	-	-
Total for 1994 and 1995			29882	30698		

Figure in parenthesis shows reserves.

Table 44
Natural Gas

(in million cu metres)

	1992	*1993*	*1994*	*1995*	*1996*	*1997*
Kazakhstan	8112	5416	4488	5916	6397	
(20 trillion cu.m. R)	6100					
Kyrgyzstan	-	42	39	36	84	-
Tajikistan	-	2	1	1	-	-
Turkmenistan	-	-	35722	32264	35182	-
Uzbekistan	-	45034	46240	47000	-	-
Total for 1994 and 1995			86490	85217		

Figure in parenthesis shows reserves.

Source: Ministry of Commerce. Government of India Report 1996. Reference in Ahmad Mukarram's *India, Iran and Central Asia* 1997 and Ahmad Mukarram: *India, Iran and Central Asia*, 1999, Rajiv Gandhi Institute for Contemporary Studies, New Delhi, 1997.

Europa World Book, 1998 and 2004, Vol. II, pp. 1940, 2032, 3268, 3398, 3696.

Vol. II. 2004 pp. 2420, 2551, 4065, 40261, 4620.

Table 45

Crude Petroleum

(in 000 metric tonnes)

	1998	*1999*	*2000*	*2001*	*2002*
Kazakhstan	25945	26736	20648	36000	42037
Kyrgyzstan	-	-	-	75.5	75.5
Tajikistan	19400	18700	15400	15000	16000
Turkmenistan	6500	7800	7350	7719	8225
Uzbekistan	8100	8100	7500	7256	7241
Total					73378.5

Table 46

Natural Gas

(in million cu metres)

	1998	*1999*	*2000*	*2001*	*2002*
Kazakhstan	25945	26736	30648	11610	13137
Kyrgyzstan	-	-	-	32.8	30.1
Tajikistan	32.4	36.1	40.0	52.0	53.0
Turkmenistan	14000	22800	47000	51270	5339
Uzbekistan	54800	55000	55600	57000	58000
Total	76559.1				

From the above tables it will be seen that the CAS produced in 1995 about 31 million tonnes of crude oil and in 2002 it produced 73,378 million metric tonnes of crude and about 85 billion cubic metre of gas. The reserve of gas are also huge, in Turkmenistan, it is 8 trillion cubic metres and in Kazakhstan 20 trillion cubic metres.

Inspite of the huge resource potential, the CAS do not possess necessary investment capital nor technology to exploit it. CAS being landlocked, the major problem is to establish linkage with the outside world. Access to sea is possible through Iran. Iran since 1990 has been building a railway line between Bafq and Bandar Abbas.[6] Bafq is a small town, near Yazd, in Central Iran and the distance between Bafq and Bandar Abbas (near St of Hormuz on Persian Gulf) is about 500 km. Meashhad which is linked with Tehran and Bafq is almost the last important town connected by road with Tehran and thus the road-rail link may provide access to CAS to Indian Ocean. Another link to the west could be through Iran and Turkey. Pipe technology underneath the Indian ocean between Bandar Abbas and Mumbai could be another linkage. The land linkage between Turkmenistan, Tajikistan/Uzbekistan and India via Afghanistan and Pakistan may be feasible in the present political scenario. Another possibility could be that gas be filled in containers and transported overland up to Bandar Abbas and from there brought to India by ship.

India on its part has provided credit facilities to the tune of 60 million US dollars to all the CAS,[7], with possibilities of additional credits to be extended. Indian private firms have setup over 50 joint venture in trading and manufacturing activities in various fields including pharmaceuticals and consumer goods. However, there is considerable scope for India to take more active participation in the reconstruction and development of CAS.

Mineral Wealth

The CAS, particularly Kazakhstan, are very rich in mineral, e.g., copper, lead, zinc, silver, chrome, nickel, molybdenum, coal, salt, antimony, gold, tin phosphorities and bauxite Table 47. The discovery and location of the mineral were accomplished when the CAS were part of the erstwhile Soviet Union. The need is that there should be a thorough geological exploratory survey which will bring to light more reserves of minerals, beside, further petroleum and gas reserves may be discovered.

India has an old, well established geological survey organization with competent technical staff. It would be worthwhile if a thorough geological survey of these states in cooperation with India is organized to discover the new mineral resources and subsequently mechanism be evolved for their exploration and suitable infrastructure be developed for their export and establishment of industries based on the minerals.

Industrial Development

There are certain products which are produced in all the states, e.g., wheat flour, cotton yarn, cotton textile and footwear. Kazakhstan produced 4.0 million tonnes of pig-iron and 4.7 million tonnes of crude steel in 2002. Kyrgyzstan produced about half a million tonnes of cement (2002), Tajikistan produced knitted wool carpets and rugs to the tune of 0.4 million sq metres in 1999.

Table 47

Mineral Production

(in 000 metric tonnes)

Countries	*1988*	*1999*	*2000*	*2001*	*2002*
Kazakhstan					
Copper	339	374	430	34872	36268
Nickel	6000	-	3000	-	6314
Lead	30	34	39	5740	-
Manganese	399	363	720	-	-
Bauxite	3477	3607	3730	-	-
Zinc	224	270	320	5740	6314
Chromite	1600	2406	2007		-
Uranium (metric tonnes)	1074	1367	1740	-	-
Gold (kg)	18100	20236	28171	-	-
Tajikistan (metric tonnes)	800	800	801	-	-
Uzbekistan (metric tonnes)	-	9100	91000	85.4 (metric tonnes)	-
Uranium	2000	2150	2054	-	-
Gold (kg)	80,000	60028	62276	-	-

Turkmenistan produced woven silk fabrics, 54,529 million sq metres, woven woolen fabric 2.5 million sq metres, and about 24,000 blankets (2002), knitted wool carpets about 1 million sq metre about one million tonnes of mineral fertilizers and 0.75 million tonnes of cement (2004).Uzbekistan produced in 2002, 360 million sq metres of woven cotton fabrics, 3.7 million sq metres of woven cotton fabrics, 3.7 million of cement and 36 million KWh of electrical energy.

Turkey has established over seven hundred industrial and commercial companies within the region. Most of these Turkish firms belong to the private sectors. China is looking for a market for its industrial products, while American and European companies are moving fast to secure a foothold in the region, independently and in collaboration with Russia.

India is a secular democracy, so are the CAS. All the republics have declared secularism as their state policy. So India should evolve a policy of coordination and trade with CAS without delay. India does produce many things which CAS need and CAS produce many things in which India would be interested.

Table 48

Meat Production, 2002

(in 000 metric tonnes)

Type	*Kazakhstan*	*Kyrgyzstan*	*Tajikistan*	*Uzbekistan*	*Turkmenistan*
Beef and Veal	297.0	89.1	15.5	394	67
Mutton	93.9	41.5	14.2	82	57
Goat meat	7.2	3.8	2.1	-	03
Poultry meat	36.1	4.5	2.1	16.1	05
	434.2	147.9	40.9	492.1	132
Grand total 1707					

Source: Europa World Book, 2004, Vol. 2, pp. 1939, 2032, 3268, 3696, 3398.

Table 48 shows the production of meat of individual states as well as the total production of all the states. The Central

Asian states produce more than one million tonnes of meat. Of the total production a little less than half the production is from Kazakhstan and about half is contributed by Uzbekistan. There is considerable scope for building up an export market in the countries of Middle East and North Africa. The cattle should be fed by giving them feeds with supplements of molasses and urea.

One of the major hurdles in the production of wholesome meat under hygienic conditions lies in the primitive conditions of slaughter houses. The suggestion is that a meat complex in Kazakhstan and Uzbekistan, which produce large quantities of meat be built, and before doing so a techno-feasibility report for this modern complex be prepared on the basis of a detailed guidelines. Based on the cost estimates, modern abattoirs be set up. India has prepared such feasibility reports for setting up three modern abattoirs of different sizes and the CAS could do so in consultation with India.

By-products

Utilization of animal by-products and animal wastes is extremely vital and these aspects have received adequate attention in CAS and there is considerable loss on this score. In view of the export of hides, timely collection and improvement of their quantity is necessary. Cold storage facilities for preserving raw hides and skins are necessary.

Bones

Bones constitute a very important by-product of meat industry. Bones are crushed by mills and converted into bone meal for utilization as fertilizers.

Animal Fats

There is considerable wastage of animal fat due to non-collection or delay in collection. Full utilization of animal fats which are available in large quantities from fallen and slaughtered animals is very important. This will save millions of dollars which are being spent at present for the import of animal fat. Kazakhstan imported animal and vegetable fats to the tune of 14 million US dollars in 1994. In fact, the suggestion is that all slaughter houses in CAS should be modernized and have a by-product plant within their precincts so that all available fats from slaughtered animals could be processed.

Blood

Blood should not be wasted in the slaughter houses. Suitable arrangement be made for its collection. It should be noted that blood has several important uses. It is used extensively for industrial purposes and also as a fertilizer. Uncollected blood in a slaughter house becomes a serious sanitary problem.

Horns and Hoofs

The wastage in the collection of horns and hoofs should be eliminated. Horn and Hoofs have great value as fertilizers after conversion into meal. The horn is rich in ossein which is used in developed countries for manufacturing gelatine. The CAS can increase the export of these items.

Fallen Animals

The Ford Foundation sponsored an agricultural production Team in India in 1959 which stated that failure to make use of the carasses of fallen animals is responsible for an enormous wastage of otherwise useful material. The recommendation of the team is fully applicable to CAS. It recommended that desiccating plants fully equipped to process animal carcasses should be established on a regional basis.[8] Each state should establish a number of carcass utilization and hide flaying centre with a view to preventing the huge waste taking place. Table 49 shows the animal population in the CAS.

Table 49
Animal Population (2002)

(in 000)

	Kazakh-stan	*Kyrgyz-stan*	*Tajikis-tan*	*Uzbeki-stan*	*Turk-menistan*	*Total*
Cattle	4282	970	1091	860	5400	12603
Buffaloes	09	-	-	-	-	-
Pigs	1124	87	-	45	90	-
Sheep & Goat	10479	3744	2906	6375	9050	-
Poultry	21279	3254	1320	4800	14500	-

Source: Europa World Book, 2004, Vol. II, pp. 1939, 2032, 3268, 3397, 3696.

It will be seen that the number of cattle in CAS is a little over 12.6 million and about half of them are in Uzbekistan and one-third in Kazakhstan. Exact data are not available as to how many carcasses of fallen animals can be made available but it can be surmised that not more than half would be utilized and the remaining ones might be wasted. The economic loss due to non-utilization and underutilization of carcasses per annum is substantial. There is urgent need to establish modern carcass utilization centres. Around 50 to 60 per cent are being partly utilized and the rest are completely wasted. Proper and free utilization of animal carcasses would produce valuable sources of mineral and protein supplements to feed poultry and cattle. The quality of hides and skins would improve and boost the trade in leather and leather goods.

Oil and Gas

For the development of Central Asian economies, India and Iran can make important contribution: (a) for the development of oil, gas and mineral resources, (b) setting up of telecommunication network, (c) building up of hotels and tourist resorts, (d) human resource development particularly specialized education and public health, (e) banking and insurance, (f) rural agro-based industries, (g) small, medium scale manufacturing industries, e.g., textile, wool, silk, leather and pharmaceutical, canning and packaging, (h) transport and travel routes, and (i) computer software. Strong bilateral relations could also be developed.[9]

CAS have to reorganize their economies. For a long time they played a second fiddle to the Russian economy as suppliers of minerals and raw materials. They need now to build new economic structures and institutions and along with their relations with Russian economies, they have to find alternative sources of economic cooperation.

Dairy Development

The CAS have great scope for dairy development. There are 12 million cows in CAS and they produced in 2002, 10 million tonnes of milk which is inadequate. The breed of the cows needs to be improved.

In India, the National Dairy Development Board conceived 'Operation Flood' project, the world's biggest milk drive. The aim is to enhance milk production as well as to establish a proper marketing system. 'Operation Flood' is an integrated dairy development programme. In India it has helped about 10 million farmers through a large number of cooperative societies. These societies procured more than 10 million kg of milk per day during 1992-93. This has led the farmers to take up dairying as a subsidiary occupation. The remarkable contribution of the 'Operation Flood Project' is that the milk production in India which had been static at around 20 million tonnes in the beginning of operation flood in 1976 increased to 60 million tonnes in 1992-93 and the per capita availability of milk has also increased from 107 grams per day in 1976 to 186 grams per day in 1993.

There is need to improve the breed of the cows, increase substantially the production of milk and increase the purchasing power of the farmers with dairy development and per capita availability of milk per day. India which has valuable experience in this field may be of assistance to CAS if the cooperation is sought.

Poultry Development

Poultry is a very important component of the farmers' economy. It provides additional income as well as job opportunities. India produced about 23 billion eggs in 1993.[10] CAS had in 1994 about 218 million birds. The need is to establish poultry breeding farms which may engage themselves in poultry breeding programme and develop high egg producing hybrid and fast growing broiler strains. There is also need to establish a Central Poultry Training Institute in any one of the states to give short-term courses in poultry.

Development of Inland Fisheries

CAS produce a good deal of metric tonnes of fisheries per annum. Fisheries play an important role in the economy as it helps to increase the food supply, generates employment, raises nutritional level. The production can be substantially increased. Kazakhstan and Turkmenistan together produce three-fourths of the total catch of inland fisheries of Central Asian states. Two new innovations could be introduced to develop inland fisheries: (1) Fish Farmers Development Agency (FFDA), and (2) National Programming for Fish Seed Development (NPFSD). These organizations would help in augmenting the production of inland fisheries.

Food Processing Industries (Fruits and Vegetables)

CAS produce a variety of fruits and vegetables. Table 50 shows the production of fruits and vegetables for the year 2002.

It will be seen from Table 50 that a large variety of fruits and vegetables are produced in CAS. Food processing is important for diversification and commercialization of agriculture, for improving the rural income and rural employment. In the era of economic liberalization, CAS should invest into food processing sector and encourage exports.

Through food processing CAS can conserve and make effective utilization of fruits and vegetables. Processed fruits and vegetables can also earn foreign exchange.

Table 50

Production of Fruits and Vegetables (2002)

(in 000 metric tonnes)

Items	*Kazakh-stan*	*Kyrgyz-stan*	*Tajiki-stan*	*Turkmeni-stan*	*Uzbeki-stan*	*Total*
Fruits						
Grapes	26.3	17.7	1000	130	570	844.0
Apple	110.5	115.2	75	2	500	820.7
Pears	9.6	-	-	-	23	62.6
Apricots	14.9	30.0	-	-	43	87.9
Peaches	-	10.0	18	-	45	73.0
Plums	12.5	-	12	-	100	124.5
Cabbages	321.8	103.1	43	30	900	1424.9
Tomatoes	448.9	183.5	202	150	1000	1849.4
Cucumbers	257.4	170.0	-	-	250	677.4
Onion	309.9	131.9	148	50	150	789.8
Carrots	214.5	126.7	32	35	150	558.2
Other vegetables	15.0	76.3	51	31	311	484.3

Source: FAO, Year Book, *Production 2004*, Vol. 48, Rome.

CAS need technology for processing. India has developed technology to process all types of fruits and vegetables. Important processed items are: (a) fruit pulps and juices, (b) canned fruits and vegetables, and (c) fruit juice concentrates.

Perhaps, each of the CAS may create a directorate which may lay down product specification and other requirements for quality control on production and marketing of processed fruits and vegetables. In fact labelling and marketing requirements have to be prescribed to protect the interest of consumers. Rules have to framed to ensure the hygienic conditions for food processing. Periodic inspection of the units is to be carried out by the technical staff in order to ensure that the quantity specification and hygienic conditions are maintained. Random samples of processed fruits and vegetables have to be drawn from the factory to exercise check on quality according to the specification issued by the directorate.

Fruits which can be processed in some of the states are apple, grapes, pears, peaches, apricots and plums. While the vegetables for processing are cabbage, tomatoes, onion and potatoes.

A serious bottleneck in the expansion of fruit and vegetable processing industry is the procurement of suitable containers at reasonable prices. Glass and tin containers are important. Glass containers are used for packing products like jams, jellies, pickles, tomatoes products and beverages. Tin cans are manufactured from tin coated steel plates. Plastic containers could be used where heat sterilization for preservation is not necessary. Their cost is comparatively lower than that of glass or tin containers. About 40 per cent of the fruits in the market are either undersize, deformed or damaged. Such defects reduce the visual appeal for table purposes but their quality as food is not affected. Such fruits are quite suitable for jam, jelly and pulp preparation. If fruits, discarded for table purposes, could be separated through grading, they could be made available for the processing at cheaper rates. It is necessary to introduce compulsory grading of fruits and vegetables. It would also be necessary to locate the processing unit near the market site.

Cereals and Processing Industries

There is a wide fluctuation in the production of wheat in Kazakhstan: in 1992 it produced 18 million tonnes of wheat, but in 1993 production came down to 11.5 million tonnes and in 1994 it was 9 million tonnes. Its production of wheat flour was about 2 million tonnes in each of these years. In Turkmenistan wheat production varied between 0.5 and 0.8 million tonnes and the production of flour was about half a million tonnes. The position of Tajikistan is similar to that of

Turkmenistan. Uzbekistan and Kyrgyzstan do not produce wheat flour.

Kazakhstan in particular and other states in general can develop bakery industry. They can manufacture a number of products like bread, biscuits, buns cakes, corn, wheaties, noodles macaroni, porridge, malt syrup and other malted products. These are items of daily consumption. As bakery and confectionary articles have gained wide popularity, there is need for the establishment of modern bakery units.

Rice can be used for preparing flaked rice, puffed rice and popped rice. Modern methods be introduced for their production. Malt syrup and other malted products are nutritious and can be prepared from barley and small millet. The technical knowhow for their manufacture is available in India.

Kazakhstan produces soyabean ranging from 6 to 12 thousand tonnes per annum. Soyabean is a very rich source of protein and fats. Its flour is used in the manufacture of bakery products, snacks and foods of high protein content and Kazakhstan may take steps for its use in bakery products.

All the CAS grow roots and tubers. Kazakhstan produces between 2 and 2.5 million tonnes. Tuber crops can be used for the manufacture of industrial starch. As tuber crops cannot be kept for long, preparation of industrial starch and sago should be encouraged. Sago has great potentiality of utilization. The possibility of export of industrial starch and sago may be explored.

Agro-industries corporations be established in the states and they should participate in processing and manufacturing activities relating to agro-based products. The sphere of activity should be: (a) agricultural processing industry, (b) preservation industry relating to perishable commodities, and (c) promotion of selected agro-based industries.

The agro-industries corporation in any state should not compete with private entrepreneurs or cooperative enterprises but they should render all possible help to such units particularly those functioning on a small and medium scale. The corporations should take up those activities which have not been covered by other units. The corporation should also spread the agro-processing activities in inaccessible areas.

Notes

1. Lydolph, Paul E., *Geography of the USSR*, New York, 1970, p. 415.
2. Ibid.
3. Stamp, L.D., *Our Developing World*, London, 1952.
4. Lydolph, Paul E. (1970), *Geography of the USSR*, New York, pp. 415-420.
5. Kotlyakov, V.M., "The Aral Sea Basin", *Environment* (January, February 1991), Vol. 33, Number 1, Washington D.C.
6. Gudadhubli,R.G., "Economic Transformation in Central Asia" in Ahmad Mukarram, *India, Iran and Central Asia: Delineating Future Economic Relations*, New Delhi, p. 29.
7. Ministry of Commerce, Government of India Report 1996, Reference in Ahmad Mukarram's, *India, Iran and Central Asia* 1997, p. 29 and *Europa*, V. II
8. Report of the National Commission on Agriculture, government of India (1976), Vol, VII, p. 514.
9. Ahmad Mukarram, *Indian, Iran and Central Asia*, Rajiv Gandhi Institute for Contemporary Studies, New Delhi, p. 7.
10. FAO Year Book *'Production'*, Vol. 48, 2004.

11

India's Relations with Central Asian States

At an international conference on Central Asia held at Aligarh (India) 1970, the President of the then Indian Council for Cultural Relation, said: "From times immemorial, our history has been inextricably bound up with that of Central Asia. With indomitable courage and in quest for knowledge and adventure, saints and seers, students and teachers, artists and traders have travelled widely through the ages and contributed to the cross fertilization of cultures in this region. Streams of cultures have floated into India and have been absorbed producing the rich culture which is India today. Recent researches indicate that the Aryans first met the Dravids at Khwarizm and at the Indus valley. After the waves of Aryans converged on India, came the Greeks, followed by Huns, Afghans, Turks and the Mongols. They all took almost the same routes and they all had their roots in Central Asia."

India's cultural relation with the Central Asian lands can be studied at four levels in the historic perspective:

1. Relation in the prehistoric and protohistoric period.
2. Relation in the ancient period.
3. Relation in the medieval period.
4. Relation in the modern and contemporary period.

Prehistoric and Protohistoric Period

India had cultural contacts with Central Asian States (CAS) during the Buddhist time. There have been frequent contacts between the people of India and Central Asia particularly by the migration of ancient tribes with different technical stone cutting traditions. In the Mesolithic period the ancient route called the 'silk Route' led to the mingling of ideas and cultures. The Silk Route emanating from China, skirts the Tarim basin and the route bifurcates to north and south of the Taklamakan desert of Tarim basin on the southern flank and passing through the valley of Yarkand river and its tributaries converges upon the Karakoram pass which gives access to the upper part of the valley of Indus in Ladakh. Again, through the various Himalayan passes through which Central Asia is accessible and through these routes, in the ancient times a large number of people mingled, leading to the intermixture of ideas and cultures. The routes through these passes have also been arteries of trade between India and Central Asia.

A momentous social change was brought about in the village farming communities particularly in food production, stock raising and husbandry; grinding of tools and manufacturing of pottery. The knowledge of metallurgy created new opportunities for trade in respect of raw material and finished products and led to the development of specialized craft skill between India and Central Asian countries.

Relations in the Ancient Period

In the 2nd century BC[1] when the Saka tribes migrated to north India via the Pamirs, they carried with them elements and traditions of Central Asian culture, for example, the distinctive iron swords were discovered at Taxila which apparently can be traced back to Central Asian tribes.

The ancient relations between Central Asia and India reached their zenith in the Kushan period with the rise of the Kushan empire which incorporated many territories of Central Asia and a considerable part of north India.

Medieval Period

It was in the medieval period that the social, cultural, intellectual and economic relationship between Central Asian region and India were well established. The relationship can be considered in four parts: (a) from Arab conquest of Central Asia to the overthrow of Central Asian states particularly Bukhara by Genghis Khan's conquest to the rise of Taimur; (c) from 1370 to 1526, i.e., from Taimur to Babar, the first Moghul King of India and (d) from 1526 to the middle of the 17th century - the era of the Uzbeks in Central Asia and the Moghuls in India.

India was connected with Central Asia by two routes: (1) the Gomal pass which led to Dera Ismail Khan, (2) the Kashmir routes - after crossing the Karakoram the route reached Yarq, where the routes from Ladakh, Tibet, China and India were joined by those leading to Kashghar and from Kashghar the merchants could proceed to Samark and Bukhara.[2]

It is worthwhile to note that Indian culture influenced the culture of Central Asian lands. India's culture, ideas and thoughts produced a powerful influence over Central Asia. In the early centuries of Christian era, great centres of Buddhism appeared at Khotan, Kashghar, Tashkent and Bukhara. Later on the Caliphate at Baghdad which included Central Asia got interested in Indian science and invited Indian scholars to work in the bureau of translation; the Indian ideas got further impetus from their entry into Central Asia.

India's mathematical and astronomical ideas also found their way into Central Asia. Aryabhatta's theory that the earth rotates on its axis and Indian methods of calculation also found entry in Central Asia.

Similarly, Indian medical ideas, herbs and methods of treatment were transmitted from Baghdad to various parts of the caliphate including Central Asian states.

There was also an impact of Indian religious ideas on Central Asian states, particularly Buddhist ideas and books published in the 11th and 12th centuries. The books gave an accurate account of Buddhist psychology and doctrines. The people of Central Asia were influenced by the Indian philosophical concepts. The Karma cult, and the Indian ideas of Nirvan influenced many people in Central Asia.

The four great books, namely, those of Imam Bukhari, *Kashshaf*; *Usul* and *Hidaya*, on which the structure of Muslim religious sciences was built in India during the medieval time, came from Central Asia. At the same time, concepts of Sufism were exchanged between India and Central Asia. Although Sufism originated in Central Asia, later on India became a much stronger centre of Sufism and Central Asia looked towards India for the Sufi cult. It is interesting to note that Tashkent libraries abound in large number of Indian manuscripts of mystic work of 16th and 17th centuries.

There was free movement of people and ideas between India and Central Asian states. It was in the 11th-13th centuries that owing to the invasion of Mongols, there was an influx of people from Central Asia into India. Genghis Khan's invasion of Central Asia was devastating, as it raised to ground stately building and mosques and people sought refuge in India.

Trade also flourished between India and Central Asia during the medieval period. India produced cotton, sugar, utensils and colouring materials, while it needed from Central Asia dried fruits, pearls, precious stones and horses of good breed. The horses were particularly needed for the Indian army. Thus, there was strong social, cultural and economic relationship between India and Central Asian states.

The geo-political location of CAS is rather intriguing. It constitutes a bridge between European and Asian land masses. In the north and west lies Turkey and Russia, in the east Mongolia and China, and the south Iran, Pakistan and India. Central Asian states access to Indian ocean can only materialize through Iran, while through Turkey, a much longer route, it can have access to Europe.

A ray of hope has emerged in the rail link: Bandar Abbas-Kerman-Meshhad-Sarakh (160 km inside Iran) and its road link with Ashgabat (Ashkhabad). The road link, is of high standard, bracing all weather and rail and road link with four to six lane highway, heavy transportation is possible and provides an access to all the CAS to Indian Ocean. Further, the Kerrman-Zahidan railway in Iran at the junction of the border of Afghanistan and Baluachistan is also under construction. After its completion, CAS will be connected to Pakistan and India. There should be a comprehensive development of banking facilities to handle international transactions. A memorandum of understanding was signed by India, Iran and Turkmenistan in April 1995 which envisages movements of goods from Indian ports to the port of Bandar Abbas in Iran and from there overland to Sarakh via Meshhed (Iran) and to other Central Asian destinations.[3] CAS need quickly to build a large network of roads and railways to allow a greater and faster movement of goods and passenger.

The Iranian route shall be more reliable than the prospective route through Afghanistan and Pakistan. Iran, on the pattern of European Union (EU), has established and strengthened and expanded Economic Cooperation Organization (ECO) by encouraging the republic to join the organization which has now turned into the second largest regional Union after the European Union. Membership of the ECO covers 10 states, over 7 million sq km area, and a population of 300 million. ECO has turned into one of the richest regions of energy and agricultural raw material resources and one of the largest markets for industrial productions.

Some Indian leaders have visited the CAS, and the Presidents of CAS have also visited India. For example, in 1996, the Vice-President of India visited Kazakhstan from 20-22 September, 1996 and this was followed by a visit of the President of Kazakhstan to India from 9-11 December, 1996. As a result of these visits working groups were constituted for medium and small scale industries, peaceful use of nuclear energy and cooperation in the field of hydrocarbon. The agreement in the field of hydrocarbon also envisages exploration, development, investment for upgradation, and modernization of refineries, pipelines and training programmes.

The Vice-President of India visited Kyrgyzstan from 18-20 September, 1996. In 1997, President A. Niyazov of Turkmenistan visited India on 25-26 February and a memorandum of understanding was signed between the Prime Minister of India and the President of Turkmenistan.

A series of bilateral agreement have been signed. Under these agreements India has offered Uzbekistan management consultancy and credit of 10 million US dollars. In 1993, India signed five agreements with Tajikistan on trade, economic cooperation, banking, culture and sports and a credit of 5 million US dollars. India and Tajikistan have signed a number of agreements during the visit of Turkman delegation to India and the Indian Prime Minister to Ashgabat (Ashkhabad) in September 1995, while in March 1995, India extended a credit of 5 million US dollars to Turkmenistan for buying pharmaceutical products which was supplemented by a further credit of 10 million US dollars in September 1995. India has extended credits to Kazakhstan and Kyrgyzstan.[4]

Although India's cooperation with the CAS has been of a high order compared to Pakistan, Iran, China and Turkey, still the investment is not very significant. There are many bottlenecks for private Indian business men to make investment in the CAS owing to: (a) lack of transport facilities, (b) political uncertainties, (c) low profit margin, and (d) low income level of the local population. However, it is in the interest of CAS and India that India should launch vigorously cultural, political and economic initiatives in the CAS.

A very encouraging factor for strengthening the relationship between India and CAS is that the CAS, though predominantly Muslim, have declared secularism as the policy of the states. It is in conformity with the policy of India and the relations can be further strengthened.

A problem which may bother CAS, arising out of their geostrategic location, is their security, particularly that of Tajikistan. President Imamali Sharipovich Rahmonov of Tajikistan declared his opposition to Islamic fundamentalism. There was great opposition to his policies and there ensued a civil war and a very large number of Tajiks crossed the border to live in Afghanistan as refugees. It is alleged that the Taliban regime in Afghanistan based on Islamic fundamentalism is aiding the opposition in Tajikistan. Tajikistan has asked for military assistance from Russia and a collective security treaty was signed in Tashkent in May 1992 and there are more than 2,500 Russian troops which are guarding the 1,300 km long Tajik-Afghan border.[5]

The problem of Uzbekistan is that of management. Uzbekistan is the fourth largest producer of cotton in the world. The monoculture has affected the fertility of land. Heavy use of chemicals without any green manuring has reduced the yield year after year. The removal of subsidies has led to inflation.

CAS need land reform which may ensure land rights for the people as about half the population depends on the land.

It may be pointed out that Kazakhstan needs specialized machines, light engineering goods and food processing industries. A good cooperation can be built up in helping Kazakhstan and other Central Asia Republics in developing food processing technology. Kazakhstan is in need of information technology and India has the competitive edge at the international level.

What is embarrassing to note is the observation of Prof. Ramnath Narayan Swamy of the Indian Institute, Bangalore that during his many visits in the past two year (1996 and 1997) he found major teams of businessmen from Turkey, South Korea, Hongkong, Pakistan, Japan, China, and western Europe, but a conspicuous absence of Indian businessmen in these countries.[6]

Indian's stock of prestige is high in Central Asian states for various reasons: (a) it is a country respected for her traditional wisdom and rich culture heritage; (b) it is a modern parliamentary democracy with vibrant political ethos; (c) in matters of foreign policy, it has a non-aligned position; (d) it is secular, multi-ethnic, multi-lingual; (e) it is multi-religious, secular country having a sizeable Muslim population, more than twice that of Central Asia; (f) it has the foundation of modern industry and a huge pool of skilled manpower; (g) in the field of agriculture its progress is spectacular; and (h) it is a country with historic roots of relation with CAS.

However, India's investment in CAS as compared with Pakistan, Iran, China and Turkey is not significant. Indian private businessmen have not entered in the CAS in a big way. It might be (a) due to lack of transportation facilities, (b) low profit margins, and (c) poor infrastructure facilities and low income level of the population.[7] However, the private sector along with government initiative have to be encouraged to invest in CAS.

It will thus be seen that the development of Central Asia is a tripartite game: India, Iran, and CAS. Central Asian states are landlocked. The biggest problem is to find a safe, secure, easy and quick means of transport for mutual trade transaction between India and CAS. In this regard Iran would be the key player. Iran has 800 km long border in the Indian Ocean from Bandar Abbas to Chahlehar and Iran is building up five New

Economic Zones there. Iran is further connecting its railway network to Pakistan and from there it can be connected to India. Through Mashhad, Iran is already connected with Turkmenistan and from there to other Central Asian states.

The CAS constitute a rich storehouse of petroleum and natural gas. Kazakhstan's 2002 production of crude petroleum was 42 million metric tonnes and that of natural gas about 13 billion cubic metre; Turkmenistan in 2002 produced about 8 million metric tonnes of crude petroleum and 53 billion cubic metres of gas and Uzbekistan in 2002 produced about 72 million tonnes of crude petroleum and 58 billion cubic metres of gas in 2002. The transport of gas and crude oil from CAS can be bought to India through pipeline technology from Chahbar in Iran to India via Pakistan; if the relation between the two countries become normal, the transport of gas and oil would become possible.

Iran has the second largest reserves of natural gas in the world. The total reserves are estimated at 812 trillion cubic ft, but the annual production is nearly 1.9 trillion cubic ft (1998).

Further, Turkmenistan which has large reserve of gas also desires an outlet to the Arabian Sea. Other states of CAS having reserves of gas would also like to be a partner in this venture.

Ashgabat, capital of Turkmenistan is connected with the Iranian town of Mashhad with a good weather road. Mashhad is connected with Tehran with a good road. From Tehran a good weather road leads to Bafq near Yazd and Bafq is joined by railway to Bandar Abbas on the Gulf coast. At some distance on the Iranian coast near Pakistan border, lies the town of Chahbahar.

Today, Iranian exports of gas go to India by sea tankers. Iran approached Pakistan Government for transit rights for an Iran-India overland pipeline. Pakistan, it is reported, has accepted the request on the understanding that Pakistan would receive transit fee between US $ 600-700 million. The pipeline would also serve as an outlet for export of gas by the CAS.

Figure 22

Proposed Over Land Gas Pipe Line Between Iran and India Through Pakistan

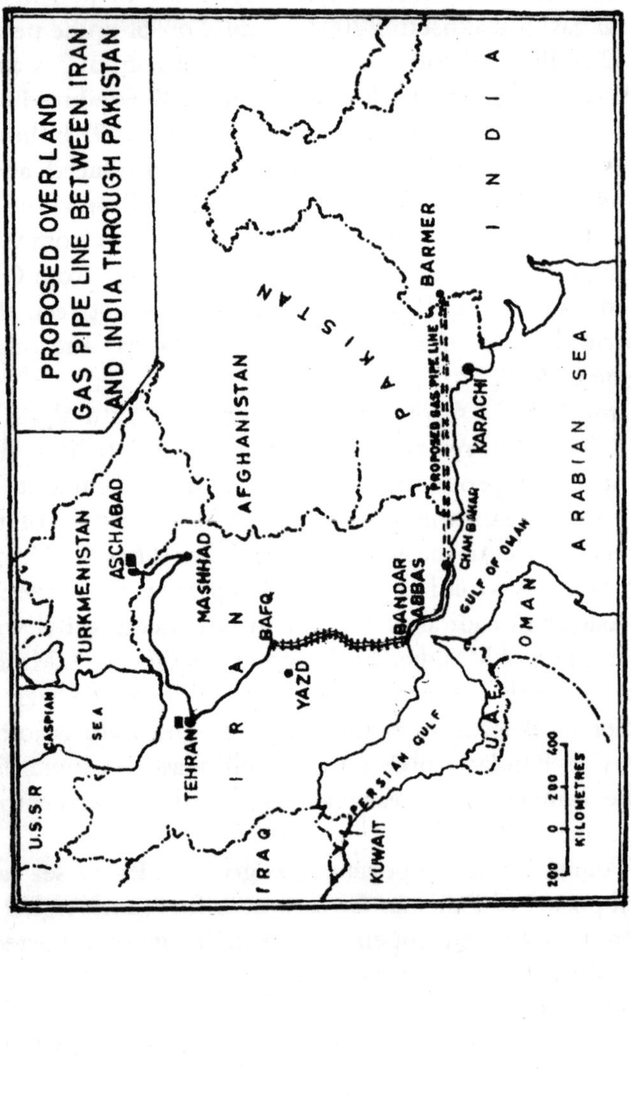

Source: Britannica Atlas 1977 and Survey of India, *School Atlas* 1964.

There is also a suggestion that the overland Iran-India pipeline may form the nucleus of an elaborate grid for Qatar, UAE and Oman with possible sub-sea link (Figure 22).

Another article of export is cotton. Uzbekistan produced 1.3 million tonnes of cotton in 1995 and Turkmenistan in the same year produced 0.4 million tonnes. India may well import cotton via Iran by ship.

Other areas of cooperation between India and CAS are in the fields of manufacturing and construction. These sectors are not well developed in any of the states. In Kazakhstan, they employ 15 and 11 per cent respectively. In Uzbekistan, it is 15 and 6.6 per cent respectively; in Turkmenistan it is 10 and 12.5 per cent respectively. In Tajikistan it is 12 and 8.7 per cent respectively (Table 17).

India can provide the needed technology in the manufacture of cotton, wool and silk fabrics; also in the field of food processing industry, leather industry and dairy development, cement manufacture, paper, fertilizer and bakery.

It will thus be seen that there is great scope of cooperation between CAS, India and Iran, and India should strengthen its relation with CAS.

Central Asia is a huge potential market for Indian goods. India can supply to Central Asian states many useful things which these states need at reasonable prices, e.g., modern agricultural implements, machinery, transport equipment, iron and steel, engineering and sports goods, tea, coffee, jute and leather goods and softwares for computers. India can also provide middle level technologies and can also train the manpower in many fields. She can import from CAS petroleum, woven silk fabrics and gas.

It was in 1997, that India signed an agreement with Iran and Turkmenistan for the transit of goods between India, Iran and Turkmenistan via sea and land. The agreement will be helpful in respect of transport with other Central Asian states also.

Central Asia beckons India. Let India listen to it. If the opportunity slips off, it may be lost forever. Kyrgyzstan has made its currency convertible and Uzbekistan with largest market and infrastructure is also likely to do so. It would attract multinationals with funds to invest. Indians would then find the Central Asian market difficult to penetrate.

Central Asia is the fourth largest producer of cotton in the world. Cotton needs ginning and weaving. It is exported raw. There is abundance of milk requiring dairying technology since most butter and cheese are imported. The story is the same for leather and leather goods. Uzbekistan imports 90 per cent of its requirements. There may be fluctuating economic conditions but one cannot wait for the ideal conditions.

Notes

1. Stavisky, Sridnaya Aziz: *Central Asia and India*, Moscow, 1964, p. 169.
2. Nizami, K.A., *India's Cultural Relations with Central Asia During the Medieval Period in Central Asia,* (ed.) by Amlendie Guha: Indian Council for Cultural Relations, Vikas Publication, New Delhi, pp. 157-166.
3. Ahmad Mukkarram, *India, Iran and Central Asia*, RGICS, New Delhi, 1998, p. 18.
4. Dash, P.L., "Perspective Across the Pamir, Realities of Evolving Ties, in India, Iran and Central Asia", Rajiv Gandhi Institute for Contemporary Studies, project No. 23, 1998, p. 137.
5. Ibid., RGICS, p. 141.
6. Ramanath Narayan Swamy, "Opportunities for Indian Basin in Central Asia" in Ahmad Mukkaram's *India, Iran and Central Asia*, RGICS project No. 23, New Delhi, 1998, p. 137.
7. Ibid., p. 138.

Bibliography

Adamchuk, V.A. (1964), "The Problem of Creating a Kazakhstan Metallurgical Base" *Soviet Geography,* 5 (6), pp. 20-35.

Alampiev, P. (1958), *Soviet Kazakhstan*, Foreign Languages Publishing House, Moscow, pp. 180, 186.

Allworth, E. (ed.) (1967), *Central Asia: A Century of Russian Rule,* Columbia, U.P., New York.

Babayev A.G., et al. (1968), "Basic Problem in the Study and Development of Desert Territories of USSR", *Soviet Geography*, 9 (6) pp. 430-43.

Bacon, E.E. (1966), *Central Asia Under Russian Rule: A Study in Cultural Change*, Cornell U.P.

Belyayev, N.A. (1968), "Industrial Development of the Desert of West Turkmenia", *Soviet Geography* 9 (6), pp. 511-537.

Bobrov, S.N. (1961), "The Transformation of the Caspian Sea", *Soviet Geography: Review and Translation*, pp. 47-59.

Borovskiy, V.M. (1980), "The Drying out of the Aral Sea and its Consequences", *Soviet Geography,* 12, pp. 63-77.

Buyanovsk, M.I. (1965), "Balkhash, A Potential Major Industrial Complex", *Soviet Geography: Review and Translation*, pp, 5-15.

Buyanovskiy, M.I. (1961), "On the Question of Iron and Steel Plant Location in Kazakhstan," *Soviet Geography*, 2, pp. 44-56.

Clarke, R.A. (1969), "Soviet Agricultural Reform since Khrushchev", *Soviet Studies*, 20, pp. 159-178.

Cole, J. and German, F., (1970), *A Geography of the USSR*, Butterworth, London.

Conolly, V. (1967), *Beyond the Urals: Economic Development in Soviet Asia*, London,

Conolly, V. (1970), "Soviet Central Asia", pp. 377-383, in G.Schopflin (ed.), *The Soviet Union and Eastern Europe: A Handbook*, London.

Durgin, Frank A., (1962), Jr. "The Virgin Lands Programme 1954-60", *Soviet Studies*, pp. 255-280.

Feygin, L.Ya, (1964), "Problems of Improving Inter-Regional Productive Relationships of the Central Asian Economic Regions", *Soviet Geography*, 5 (6), pp. 3-10.

Field Neil C., (1954), "Amu Darya: A Study in Resource Geography", *Geographical Review*, pp. 528-542.

Garbutt, R., (1950), *Russian Railways*, London.

Geller, S.U. (1962), "On the Question of Regulating the Level of the Caspian Sea", *Soviet Geography*, pp. 59-66.

Geller, S.U. (1964), "The Transformation of Nature and the Development of Natural Resources of Arid Areas", *Soviet Geography*, 5 (6), pp. 34-42.

Gerasinov, I.P., (1968), "Basic Problems of the Transformation of Nature in Central Asia", *Soviet Geography*, 9, pp. 444-458.

Gerasinov, I.P., Armand, D.L. and Yefron, K.M., (eds.) (1971), *Natural Resources of the Soviet Union, their Use and Renewal*, Translation ed. W.A.D., Jackson, Freeman, San Francisco.

Hahn, W.G. (1972), *The Politics of Soviet Agriculture*, 1960-1970, London.

Hooson, D.J.M., (1964), "A New Soviet Heartland", *The Geographical Journal*, pp. 19-29.

Jackson (1956), W.A. Douglas, "The Virgin and Idle Lands of Western Siberia and Northern Kazakhstan: A Geographical Appraisal", *Geographical Review*, pp. 1-19.

Karsten A.A. (1963), "The Virgin Lands and its prospects of Development", *Review and Translation*, pp. 37-46.

Khan, A.R. and Ghai, D. (1970), *Collective Agriculture and Rural Development in Soviet Central Asia*, London.

Kornilov, B.A. and Timoshkina, V.A. (1975), "The Impact of Karakum on the Environment", *Soviet Geography*, 16, pp. 308-314.

Kuznetsov, N.T. (1977), "Geographical Aspects of the Future of the Ara Sea", *Soviet Geography*, 18, pp. 163-171.

Laird, R.D. and Crowley, L. (eds.) (1965), *Soviet Agriculture, the Permanent Crisis*, New York,

Lavishchev, A. (1969), *Economic Geography of the USSR*, Moscow.

Lewis, Robert A. (1962), "The Irrigation Potential of Soviet Central Asia", Annals of the Association of American Geographers, pp. 99-114.

Lewis, Robert A. (1966), "Early Irrigation in West Turkestan", *Annals of the Association of American Geographers*, pp. 467-491.

Lovrich, M.I. (1977), "Geographical Aspects of Territorial Redistribution of Water Resources in the USSR", *Soviet Geography*, 18, pp. 557-574.

Luknitsky, Pavel (1954), *Soviet Tajikistan*, Foreign Languages Publishing House, Moscow, p. 264.

Lydolph, Paul E. (1970), *Geography of the USSR., New York, pp. 217-296.*

Mathieson, R.S. (1975), *The Soviet Union, an Economic Geography*, London.

Matley, I.M. (1970), "The Golodnaya Steppe: A Russian Irrigation Venture in Central Asia", *Geographical Review*, 60 (3), pp. 328-346.

Mecauley, M. (1976), *Khrushehev and the Development of Soviet Agriculture: The Virgin Land Programme*, 1953-64, London.

Mellor, R.E.H. (1964), *Geography of the USSR*, London.

Micklin, P.P. (1978), "Irrigation Development in the USSR During the 10th Five-Year Plan (1976-1980)" *Soviets Geography*, 19 pp. 1-24.

Mikhailov Nicholas (1948), *Soviet Russia: The Land and its People*, New York.

Mikhailov, N.N. (1950*), Soviet Land and People*, London.

Nikolskiy, I.V. (1961), "The Geography of Transportation of Kazakhstan", *Soviet Geography* 2 (3), pp. 44-54.

Nove, A., Newth, J.A. (1967), *The Soviet Middle East: A Model for Development*, New York.

Pavlenko, V.F. (1963), "The Transport Geography Situation and the Interregional Links of Central Asia", *Soviet Geography*, 4, pp. 27-33.

Prodst Aye, (1964), "Further Productive Specialization of the Central Asian Region", *Soviet Geography* 5 (6), pp. 11-20.

Pryde, P.R. (1968), "The Areal Deconcentration of the Soviet Cotton Textile Industry", *Geographical Review*, 58, pp. 575-921.

Rakowska-Harmstone, T. (1969), *Russia and Nationalism in Central Asian, The Case of Tajikistan*, Baltimore.

Ryazanstev, S.N. (1951), *Kirghizia*, Foreign Languages Publishing House, Moscow.

Schuyler, E. (1966), *Turkistan*, G. Wheeler (ed.), London.

Shabad, Theodore (1963), *Geography of the USSR: A Regional Survey*, New York. P. 334-408.

Shaffer, H.G. (1977), *Soviet Agriculture, An Assessment of its Contribution to Economic Development*, New York.

Skosyrev, P. (1956), *Soviet Turkmenistan*, Foreign Languages Publishing House, Moscow.

Skosyrev, Perr G. (1956), *Soveit Turkmenistan*, Foreign Languages Publishing House, Moscow, pp. 231.

Soviet News (1950), *The Sixteen Republics of the Soviet Union*, London.

Spring, D. (1975), "Railways and Economic Development in Turkestan before 1917" in Symons and White, (eds.), pp. 46-74.

Strauss, E. (1969), *Soviet Agriculture in Perspective*, London.

Strauss, E. (1970), "The Soviet Dairy Economy", *Soviet Studies*, 21, pp. 269-296.

Symons Leslie, et al. (1983), *The Soviet Union: A Systematic Geography*, London.

Symons, L. (1972), *Russian Agriculture, a Geographical Survey*, London.

Taaffe, R. (1960), "Rail Transportation and Economic Development of Soviet Central Asia", University of Chicago Research paper No. 64,

Taaffe, R. (1962), "The Transportation and Regional Specialization: The Example of Soviet Central Asia", Annals of the Association of American Geographers, 52, (1), pp. 80-98.

Taskin. G.A. (1954), "The Falling Level of the Caspian Sea in Relation to Soviet Economy", *Geographical Review*, October, pp. 508-527.

Tikhomirov (1961), *Cities of Central Asia*, Central Asian Research Centre, London.

Vitkorich, Voctor (1954), *The Tour of Soviet Uzbekistan*, Foreign Languages Publishing House, Moscow, p. 246.

Westwood, J.N. (1963), *Soviet Railways To-day*, London.

Whecler, G. (1965), *The Modern History of Soviet Central Asia*, London, 1965.

Whitletl Giles (1993), *Central Asia: The Practical Handbook*, Connecticut USA.

Williams, D.S.M. (1967), "The City Of Tashkent; Past and Present", *Royal Central Asian Journal*, 54 (1), pp. 33-43.

Zaytoev, M.K. (1968), "The Development of the Oil and Gas Industries of Turkenia", *Soviet Geography*, 9 (6), pp. 503-10.

Index